THE
GENTLE
SOLDIER
A WWI STORY

JOYCE ENGELBERT

AuthorHouse™
1663 Liberty Drive
Bloomington, IN 47403
www.authorhouse.com
Phone: 1 (800) 839-8640

Published by AuthorHouse 02/04/2019

ISBN: 978-1-5462-7402-5 (sc)

Library of Congress Control Number: 2018915222

Print information available on the last page.

authorHOUSE®

I wrote this book about my father, who was in World War One. He was in the first group of American soldiers to land on French soil in 1917. It was a heart wrenching time for him. His efforts as a medic, who was pressed into service as an infiltrator and interpreter under the leadership of General Pershing earned him many awards and medals from the French Government.

This story is about a gentle, classical pianist who became very important in the war. I had taken a writing class at our local Senior Center, and have really enjoyed writing this story. My class urged me to take it as far as I can. I hope you enjoy it

CHAPTER 1

CH ENGELBERT

CH came down the gangplank and set foot on French soil. St.Nazaire to be exact. It had been selected as the port of debarkation. As one of thousands of soldiers coming ashore that day in 1917, he was slightly bewildered as French bands were playing, and American bands were playing. The Mayor of St. Nazaire was welcoming all the soldiers at the top of his lungs. Soon the men were being marched down the road -and after about 3 miles came to the barracks they would stay in until they were dispersed to the front. They all did training exercises until they got their orders. The fighting methods of the enemy were so brutal, that new training was needed. CH found himself wondering if he could do it. Shooting at targets was one thing, but real people? He wasn't so totally convinced.

The training consisted of digging trenches on stony ground, that included the typical first line, support and reserve trenches, properly protected by wire entanglements. French and British instructors explained the use of trench weapons, such as the hand and rifle grenades, the 37-mm. gun and the trench mortar. They also learned how to signal aeroplanes from the trenches, and to signal from trench to trench. Special attention was given to the use of gas masks, the different kinds and the discipline to perfect putting them on. The saying became common that when the gas alarm was given there remained only the "quick and the dead".[1]

1   History of the First Division. WW1 1917 - 1919

After what seemed like months of intense training with the French and British troops in the most extreme winter conditions that most Americans had ever experienced, which was absolutely necessary for survival in combat. As if the weather wasn't enough, they had only a sandwich and water from their canteens for a mid day meal every day.

Their morale was kept high by constantly praising their fighting spirit, stimulating confidence in their skills with weapons, and a sense of superiority over the enemy.

When not in training, the men mostly stayed in the barracks where it was somewhat warm. They wrote letters home, washed their extra socks and underwear, cleaned their equipment, rifles, other weapons, or read technical manuals. Some read the Bible, some prayed, and some slept.

CH kept his rifle meticulously clean,and the bayonet razor sharp. But then, every thing about him was like that. Meticulous. His dark hair was always combed just so, clean shaven face-some might even call handsome, with his intense blue eyes and full lips. He was tall and slender, but not frail. H e could hold his own at arm wrestling with his buddies. He had long slender fingers, and once he wrapped them around your hand, you kinda' knew you were in trouble. Those were piano hands, long, strong, nimble. He could almost stretch two octaves. He had the same stretch as Eddie Duchin. CH was proud of that.

By January 5, the last of the training was ended, and the Division was pronounced qualified to take its place in the line as a combat unit.[2] In light of this, they were given passes to go into town three miles away. A short walk after all they'd been through.

CH and four or five other Privates went together to a small cafe that advertised home cooked food. Most of the other group opted for the places that sold beer.

While at the cafe, CH heard a piano being played from another room, so he asked who was playing, and the lady said it was her 15 year old daughter Cherree, and she hated the thing and was always trying to break it. He asked politely if he could go talk to her and maybe play for her. "Oh yes monsieur, anything you can do." So he went in and asked if he could sit with her at the piano and watch her play. She usually would have refused and walked off in a huff, but there was such a kindness in his face, and gentleness in his voice that she nodded and scooted over so he could sit beside her. "What kind of music do you like to play?" he asked. "I like popular songs, but mama' likes classics", she replied. "I started playing classical music when I was very young and I still play them, but for fun, I play popular music. What ones do you know?", asked CH. "Oh, there's one I heard on the radio when we were allowed to listen to it, I think it was hmm, hmm…oh yes, Sweet Emalina!, but I don't have the music for it" she said, dropping her arms in disappointment.

"Well" said CH in his slow Indiana drawl, "I played it once or twice at home, but I don't know the words to it." and he began to play. Cherree sang what words she recalled and "La La La'd" the ones she didn't.

2   History of the First Division. WW1 1917 - 1919

Then he played another song called "I Want to be in Dixie" which brought in a couple more people who knew that song and they began singing it. Soon all of his buddies, and most of the other patrons of the little cafe were standing around the piano, eating, drinking French coffee and singing their hearts out in whatever language they spoke, to whatever music was being played. Cherree watched fascinated. Madame watched smiling. It had been a long time since both her little cafe <u>and</u> her pockets had been so full.

It was getting late and CH and the guys needed to head back to the barracks, so he played "It's a Long Way to Tipperary", which usually ended the evening, and it did. As he was leaving, Cherree touched his arm and asked "Do you think I will ever play as good as you?" To which CH replied, "If you practice every day as hard as you can on the classics and then have a friend come over while you play what you like for a few minutes, it won't seem so hard. You might even come to like it." He winked at her, tipped his hat to Cherree and her mama', turned and walked quickly into the darkness to catch up with his friends.

CHAPTER 2

Back at camp, the place was buzzing. Word was that the War General was coming in person to give the orders as to where the troops would be going. No one slept that night. In the morning,the officers and the troops were assembled for inspection. Each had their packs ready.

In the distance a motorcade was approaching the waiting troops. It stopped in front of the officers and out stepped General Pershing, and three French officers;Marshall Joffree; General Castelnau; and General Petain.

The General spoke to the assembled American Troops about how important this mission was and proud he was of each and every soldier, and how much honor they were bringing to America. CH looked at the soldiers and thought to himself, yes, we are proud, we are doing the right thing.

Then as quickly as the motorcade came, it. was was gone.

The orders had come, but were confidential,so only the officers knew where they were going. A few days later CH watched as the first group moved out. It looked liked they were going north .

The weather was terrible. Roads covered with ice and snow. By noon it had turned into a heavy downpour, then sleet. The men were loaded with their heavy packs, consisting of two blankets, emergency rations, shelter tent half, extra shoes, socks, underwear,mess equipment, and entrenching tools,in addition to the rifle, bayonet,steel helmet, two gas masks, and full ammunition belt. The heavy rain drenched them and increased the weight of their load. The wet skirts of their long overcoats clung to their legs and impeded their movements . Only a sandwich could be supplied for lunch and hunger added to the pain of the weary men. The artillery units and horses experienced the greatest difficulties from the beginning. The next day's Brigade had the same bad weather as the first .... And so it went.

Four days later the First Brigade reached the Ansauville Sector. They entered the line late at night. On March 21st, Ambulance Co. #12 relieved Ambulance Co. #13 at Mesnil-la-Tour. Their main job was getting casualties out of the trenches and back to the field hospital for treatment, and getting supplies and information back and forth. CH carried wounded out of the trenches in the rain, under the cover of gunfire. Behind some trees and piled wood, two litter bearers were waiting to carry them to safety to be treated. Sometimes if the field hospital could manage it, they would send a little food or dry socks. The ground was so low and marshy that even on the sunniest days, there was mud under foot.

While CH was sitting in a trench collecting letters from some of the soldiers, a call came from about ¾ kilometers down the trench, "Does anybody speak German? We need you now!" CH called back "I do, coming now!" as he took off in the direction of the caller. He crammed the letters inside his shirt as he hurried past other soldiers, who fired shots to cover him, and over wire that pulled at his coat. Trying to keep his head below the trench line, he half ran-half crawled his way along the slippery, mucky, smelly trench. CH arrived at a spot where three Americans and a Frenchman were holding a German soldier. "I'm private Engelbert", he said, slightly breathlessly, "I speak German, sir". "Good!", said the sergeant. "We lost our interpreter two days ago." CH looked at the German soldier and remarked, "He doesn't look so evil, he looks pretty scared." The sergeant kind of laughed and said " Yeah, I think he went out to relieve himself and got confused and jumped into our trench by mistake. They're only about 25 yards apart up near that tree, but we can't let him go."

CH: "You want me to talk to him here? Or take him back someplace safer?"

SGT: "Say something to calm him down so we can move him back."

CH (in German) "Hello, my name is Engelbert, we don't want to hurt you. If you cooperate, everything will be all right. Do you understand?"

GERMAN SOLDIER (in a calmer voice) "Name, Rank, Serial Number, Yes I understand."

As they made their way back through the muddy trench, the sergeant remarked to the Frenchman "If I hadn't seen it, I wouldn't have believed it. Engelbert has a special touch with people. Even I felt it."

They climbed out of the trench at the same spot that CH used to help the wounded. They got to the trees and then to a waiting ambulance. CH talked to the German soldier while they were in the ambulance and found out he was a private, hadn't been there very long, and didn't know anybody or anything. Also he liked to carve things out of wood with a pocket knife, and he was 16 years old.

When they got to the field headquarters, they sent the German soldier to prison camp, but they kept his uniform. The sergeant took it back with him to the trenches. While they were driving back, he talked to CH. "You remember I said that we lost our interpreter?" To which CH said, "Yes Sir."

SGT: "Well, you could be our interpreter now, you know."

CH: "Yes Sir."

SGT: "What I'm asking is more dangerous than pulling wounded out of the trenches. But you can do something more valuable for our country, France, and maybe the whole war effort. You can make a difference."

CH: "Yes sir."

SGT: "Will you do it?"

CH: "Yes Sir."

They got out of the ambulance and the sergeant handed CH the German uniform. "I think this will fit you. I sized up the prisoner and he looked about your size. We can get clean underwear and socks inside the field hospital." CH took the uniform without a word, went into the hospital, got underwear, socks and boots that fit from the pile they kept. He didn't have to ask why he was putting on the enemy's uniform. He knew.

After dark, the artillery concentrated at the other end of the trenches and the rain had turned to hail. There was so much smoke and steam that nobody saw a figure go from the tree and jump into the German trench.

CHAPTER 3

CH landed in the trench with one leg in a foot of mud and the other between the legs of a dead soldier. "Oh my God!" he gasped (in German), as gunfire whizzed overhead. Then he thought, "I sure wasn't expecting this," There was no light, except for the bursts of gunfire, heavy artillery fire, and the flame throwers. He assessed the situation as best he could. The rain was relentless. There were two dead soldiers and another one dying. The dead ones looked to be about 16, the dying one even younger. The boy was calling for his mother. CH took him, shivering, in his arms and grabbed a filthy blanket and tried to make him comfortable. The gaping hole in his chest said it wouldn't be long. CH asked if he had a letter for his mother. The boy said "N-N-No", so CH found a piece of paper and pencil in one of the packs, and wrote a short note to the boy's mother saying how much he loved his family, and to keep him in their hearts. CH got her address from the young soldier, and wrote it on the note and promised to mail it as soon as he could.

The boy seemed to find comfort when CH said, "You have made your mother proud, and she loves you very much." "Da-n-n-n-k......." and the boy was gone. CH put the note in his pocket, laid the body down, wiped his hands on the blanket, picked up his rifle and moved on down the trench. For the most part, the enemy trenches were just like he had been told. No one had much to say, mostly grunts and "Got anything to eat? Or smoke?" Gunfire was constant, incoming and outgoing. The smell was so bad that CH was constantly nauseous. He never once thought of food. He had a job to do, and do it he would.

He worked his way as far into the trench as he could without going into 'no-man's-land'. He made mental notes about everything he saw, and its position. He started using simple musical notes to distinguish artillery from mortar, and so on. He worked out a tune that contained all the information he needed to take back. It took two nights to do the leg work, and he checked the coordinates during the day. He mostly tried to be invisible.

It was his third day behind enemy lines. It was cold and rainy, turning to sleet, then back to rain again. CH was headed back to his original spot, when he suddenly heard "Halt!"

(Conversation in German)

GERMAN OFFICER: "Why are you away from your post?"

CH: "They are all dead, except for me. No one came to relieve us. I came for help before it gets dark."

GERMAN OFFICER: "Get back to your post. We'll send reinforcements!"

CH: "Yes Sir!" he saluted. Then he turned and hurried to the end of the trench where he had come in.

CH knew he couldn't leave until dark, and he didn't know how many reinforcements would be sent, so he waited. He fired his rifle into the air to appear as though he was doing his job. He piled the bodies of the dead soldiers as far away as possible. He thanked the Lord it was still winter, then he went through their sacks and took anything that might be useful.

He found ammunition for a 9mm Luger, which meant he had to search the bodies again, but then he would have a sidearm. He had to get under their muddy trench coats to feel around for the holster. He had put the youngest in the middle and was pretty sure he didn't have anything like a gun strapped on. The body on top didn't either. "I sure hope those reinforcements don't come now, " he thought, as he pushed his hand under the two bodies to check the third. One glove got stuck on a button or something and came off, so he was trying to find the gun with a bare hand. Ugh. The bodies were heavy, partly frozen and stunk, but the gun was there. He got it unbuckled and pulled it out from under the body with his foot on the stack of bodies. He wiped it as clean as he could. The Luger itself was in good condition in its holster. CH checked to see if it was loaded. It was, so he strapped it on under his overcoat. It was a little loose, but he hadn't eaten for a couple of days, so it was OK. It wouldn't fall off anyhow.

About a half hour after dark, two German soldiers came down the trench. CH had to tell them to keep their heads down. It was raining and he couldn't see their faces clearly, but he knew they were young and inexperienced. He thought to himself, "I can't shoot two boys. Dear God, what else can I do?" CH and the soldiers took their places and fired their rifles. The rain was turning to blowing snow. During a lull in the gunfire, the soldiers told CH that at 2 AM, there was going to be a rush on the enemy, and to be ready to go.

At exactly 2 AM, the two young soldiers jumped out of the trench, rifles blazing, followed by CH, crawling close to the ground. It was **chaos**. Gunfire everywhere. Soldiers running. Screaming. Falling. Crawling back to the trenches.

The snow was blowing furiously now, covering the bodies as quickly as they fell, and the bodies had fallen everywhere, strewn all over "no-man's-land". Pieces of bodies were everywhere. "This smell, the smell of war, must be what hell smells like," thought CH. With bullets whizzing every which way, he made a final dive between the two young soldiers.

CHAPTER 4

I t had been three days since CH had gone behind enemy lines. The American sergeant and the French Lieutenant had prayed silently as they watched him slip into the stormy battle ridden night. Now they were rethinking and regretting their decision to send him out so quickly. As the third day turned into afternoon, they discussed every aspect of what they told him. They had tried to familiarize him with the enemy personality close up, how their weapons worked, what their trenches were like; most importantly, what information was needed if he could get close enough to hear something. Now the afternoon was quickly fading into another gloomy, rainy night, and the barrage of artillery fire was picking up.

Midnight came and went, as did the artillery and mortar fire, grenades, flame throwers spewing death and hate into the night. Soldiers rushed the enemy line, but were cut down. By 2 AM, there was still no let up in the gunfire, but the rain was turning to snow and the wind was blowing fiercely.

Some time about 4 AM, when the weather had reached near blizzard proportions, and visibility was almost zero, one of the "dead" German soldier's eyes opened. He knew he was about 10 yards from the American trenches. He was between two bodies, He couldn't see in any direction, so he knew no one could see him.

When he went down between the two soldiers, he was pointed right toward the Allied Forces' trench. He inched his way between the bodies. As he passed the head of one of the bodies, he looked into the face of a very young man, still in his teens. The blank stare and the blood coming out of his neck said he wasn't ever getting any older. 'Somewhere there's a mother who has just lost her pride and joy.' he thought, as he inched his way closer to the trench, under the cover of the blowing snow.

Then he saw it, the familiar steel helmet with the ding in the left temple. He was less than a yard from the trench. "Hey Sarge", he whispered, "Got a match?" Eyes appeared under the brim of the helmet. "Engelbert?" "Yes sir!" Two more helmets popped up and arms pulled CH into the trench, just as a wave of gunfire took the heel off his boot. "Wow, that was close!"

CH sat in the field hospital wrapped in warm blankets while the nurses worked on his feet and hands, especially his fingers, those long slender fingers. Luckily, a little frostbite was the worst that he suffered on his first infiltration. His temperature was dangerously low, so the doctor pushed the Sergeant and the Lieutenant out, with the directive to come back in an hour!

After 55 minutes – they could wait no longer. "Doctor! We have to talk to this man. He may have vital information." CH was sipping on an endless cup of coffee. Still wrapped in blankets from head to toe, he looked like a mummy, but was up to talking, and asked for a pencil and paper.

CH took the paper, laid it on a small table and started humming. He then put down some lines and some music notes on the paper. It looked like some sort of musical map. He looked up and saw the expressions on the superiors' faces, and explained; "I couldn't write anything while I was in their trenches, so I made up a piece of music in my head, memorizing everything I saw and heard. Let me get it down on paper, then I can explain it to you. It will only take me a few minutes." He looked at them for a response. They nodded and sat on the next cot. When he finished the unusual report, CH laid the papers out in order and taped them together with hospital tape. Then he began his explanation. He had drawn a fairly accurate map of the German trench for several miles, using musical notes to pinpoint machine guns, artillery, heavy mortar, communications and underground bunker entrances and exits. "Well, what do you think so far?" CH asked. "This is good, **very** good, now that I understand it." replied the Sergeant. "They have beefed up their artillery in these areas more than we thought," as he pointed to several spots on the map. "Yes, Yes," said the Lieutenant, "we never did know exactly where the communications were. We will change our tactics tonight! We must get out the orders immediately!"

The Lieutenant stood directly in front of CH. In his sincere officer's voice, he said "Private Engelbert, you have done a great service for France today. We shall not forget!" He saluted and then hugged CH and ran off to get the orders out.

"This **is** important," said the Sergeant. "If we can knock out their communications, we can slow them down. We have more American Divisions on the way." He too saluted CH out of respect for the work he had done, turned and quickly followed after the French Lieutenant.

[33]The First Division, known as "The Big Red One" remained aggressive, conducting frequent raids. In March 1918, Secretary of War Baker of the U.S. Arrived in France to see the AEF (American Expeditionary Forces) firsthand. General Pershing acted as his escort.

After seeing the port facilities at St. Nazaire, they visited a base hospital at Savenay, and several other military sites. Then Baker and Pershing were off to the front to see the "Big Red One", where

[3]   [3]America in WWI by Goldstein and Maihafer

the 16th Infantry Regiment held a review in their honor. Just a few days earlier, **some of its members had been decorated for heroism by the French**.

9-5 Members of the the "Big Red One" Infantry Division being decorated for heroism

CHAPTER 5

Over at the Eastern Front, Russia no longer wanted to fight the Germans. They were having their own troubles. The Treaty of Brestlitovsk between Gremany and Russia was signed on March 3, 1918. That meant all the German forces could be added to the Western Front.

There was a massive attack on March 21ˢᵗ against the British 5ᵗʰ Army, which nearly crushed it. The U.S. 2ⁿᵈ Division went to their aid. On April 11ᵗʰ, General Haig issued his "Back to the Wall" order to "fight to the last man". The 26ᵗʰ (Yankee) Division saw its first serious fighting. It did not go well. Pershing was furious. The American Army needed to restore its reputation, preferably through an all American operation.

By the end of May, the AEF has 11 combat divisions in France and England. The 1ˢᵗ Division was with the French near Amiens. The other American divisions were committed elsewhere. The Village of Cantigny was selected as the objective of an assault that would demonstrate the American capability.

Pershing gave the task to his trusted 1ˢᵗ Division, "The Big Red One". Speaking directly to the officers and men, dropping his characteristic reserve, "You are going to meet a savage enemy flushed with victory. Meet him like Americans. When you hit, hit hard, and don't stop hitting. You don't know the meaning of defeat."

CH felt the emotion in the General's voice. He knew it was coming from his heart. It got him all fired up. It got all of them fired up.

On May 28ᵗʰ, after a two-hour artillery barrage, which began at 4:45 AM, the order was given to "go over the top". Supported by French tanks, machine gun fire, and a rolling artillery barrage, lines of Doughboys moved, under cover of smoke. By 7:30 AM, Cantigny was taken, but holding on to it was not easy. The enemy continued to fight fiercely. During the mopping up of the small town, there was fighting at close quarters, but the entire enemy garrison was promptly overcome and made prisoners.

The French flame-throwers were invaluable in driving the enemy out of the dugouts. As soon as the objective was reached, the artillery enclosed the captured area. Soon after the attack began, prisoners were started to the rear. In all, five officers and 225 men were captured. CH was called upon as an interpreter.

It was learned from the prisoners, that the attack came as complete surprise. None of the brave men who, earlier, fell into the hands of the Germans had given away the plans for the big assault.

The success did wonders for troop morale and to restore American prestige. It was one of the most important engagements of the war in its importance to our war-wearied and sorely tried Allies. *

* Source: <u>America in WWI</u>

Page 16

10th Army Corps.

No. 818 C.

July 4, 1918

GENERAL ORDER

The General, Officers and Men of the First Division:

Tomorrow, the first elements of your Division will depart from the area of the 10th Army Corps. In four days, you will have left us.

I am still deeply impressed by the celebration of your "independence Day" and by the magnificent show I witnessed this morning in reviewing one of your battalions and saluting the Star Spangled Banner. I wish to express to you the regret that I and all the officers and men of the 10th Army Corps feel at seeing you leave this sector where youhave shed your generous blood and earned your first success.

In this sector the French soldiers are called "The Men of Griveness" and you, Sons of America, we are happy to call "The Men of Contigny".

General, Officers and Men of the First Division:

In bidding you fartewell, I wish you the glorious fortune which your gallantry deserves.
*As war may bring us together again, I do not say "Adieu" but "Au revoir". ***

General Vandenburg,
Commanding the 10th Army Corps.

** Source: <u>History of the First Division</u>

CHAPTER 6

On July 4, after the celebration, CH and the medics began packing up supplies for a move, although they didn't know where they were going. While he was working, the sergeant came by. It was the first time since he started interpreting that he and the sergeant had a chance to talk. "Well, Private Engelbert, how are you?" he said in a pleasant voice to let CH know that this was not official.

"I'm fine. A little tired, but fine. How are you Sarge?"

"I'm just fine too, Private. I just wanted to see how you were doing since we never really did get to talk to each other. You know I don't even know your first name. You could have died out there, and I didn't know your first name."

CH smiled at that and replied,"My first name is Clarence, but my fiends call me CH."

Well CH, when we are just talking like this, you can call me Jack, but be careful with it. Some of the other armies don't like us to be friendly with each other. Some do, some don't, but anyway, I've been really curious to know some things about you. Would you mind telling me a little bit about yourself?" "Not at all, Jack. What do you want to know?" "Well for starters, how is it that you speak German so fluently? Our first interpreter did pretty good for the most part, but he got stuck a few times, and he got caught when he tried to infiltrate the German trenches."

CH's jaw dropped and his eyes got big, as he asked tentatively,"what happened to him?" Sarge saw his expression and quickly said"Oh, they took him prisoner, and sent him to a POW camp. I <u>heard</u> they use him to interpret <u>our</u> guys."

CH relaxed. That seemed to be a realistic explanation that he could accept.

"How did your first interpreter learn to speak German?" asked CH.

"I'm not completely sure, but I think he learned it in college in the U.S.," Sarge answered.

"Oh, I see. I'm sure that's a good way to learn a language, but I grew up with it. My parents were from Germany. Most of my relatives spoke it too, so by the time I was in the 2nd grade, I was equally fluent in both English and German. Since my relatives came from different parts of Germany, I learned the different dialects. I guess, because I was so young, it was easy to learn to read and write it. My home town, Richmond, Indiana, had a lot of German people coming to settle, and my mom had me go and interpret for them and read papers and things like that for them. Does that answer your question?" grinned CH.

Sarge grinned back and said with a chuckle, "Well that takes care of the language question, now how in the heck did you manage the crazy map with the musical notes for machine guns and heavy artillery? And the humming? I can't wait for <u>this</u> explanation." (still chuckling).

CH chuckled too. He knew the explanation would sound pretty funny. "OK, here goes. I learned to play the piano when I was very young, about four or five. I learned to memorize whole sonatas note by note, phrase by phrase, until I could hum it in my head. That way, I could write it down, if I was taking a test, or play it on the piano, if I was taking a test that way. As I got older, I started making a game out of it using cars, horses, houses, trees, and making them into different musical notes and humming until I'd get home, write it down, and then play it on my piano. Some times it would sound pretty good, some times, well it sounded like that heavy artillery. Who would have thought that my childhood game could come in handy some day?"

"Boy oh Boy" said the sergeant, "that is something. I don't think anybody could have figured that out after you had written it down. What a code that would make. Maybe you can teach me how to decipher it and we can use it. Let's give it some thought. See if you can write it down somehow. What the lines and notes mean, and if I can't get it, maybe another musician can," he said, as he turned to leave. "I've got to go. It was good to talk to you CH. I don't know where we are going yet, but I'll see you there."

"OK, Sarge. Thanks for stopping by," replied CH. He then finished packing supplies and put the flaps down on the bag, tied the ends, and put it with the others. He put some extra paper in his pack, thinking he would work on the musical code, just in case the sergeant was serious. Maybe since no orders had come down yet, just maybe they were going to get a rest period. They sure could use it, he thought.

CHAPTER 7

When the First Division began moving out, the men little dreamed of the momentous role that they were soon to bear, and many thought that they were en route to a rest area, but that was not to be.

The Germans had made a great drive into France and had eaten a huge pocket into the French lines that extended to the Marne River. With immense forces and munitions, they intended to advance toward Paris. The Allied troops along the Marne had checked this advance, but another assault might well overwhelm them and open the way to Paris.

General Foch, the new generalissimo, looked for an opportunity to counter-attack and regain the initiative. The opportunity came in July. The 10th French Army, commanded by General Mangin, was entrusted with the assault. The spearhead of the thrust was to be the 20th Corps under General Berdoulet.

The troops assigned to the Corps were the First American Division on the left, the First Moroccan Division in the center, and the Second American Division on the right.

It was essential that the counter-attack should begin as a surprise. Only the minimum of time was allowed to assemble the troops and they were kept in ignorance of their mission until the last possible moment.

July 11, 1918, the First Division was placed at the disposal of the 10th French Army, and ordered to the area of Dammartin-en-Goele, northeast of Paris. French truck-trains were made available for the dismounted troops. The rest were to march. The entire Division was required to move only at night and to remain in the woods or villages during the day, in order to prevent discovery by the enemy's aviators.

The field artillery and trains left the Beauvais area late in the afternoon of July 12th, and began a march that was made memorable by the hardships endured by men and animals.

As if to increase the difficulties, the weather was rainy, and the roads and fields were deep in mud. No fires were allowed and the food was cold and unpalatable. Zero Hour was to be 04:35 AM, July 18th.

The two nights before Zero Day, everything was stepped up to a rush. The roads were filled with all manner of vehicles to transport gear to the line.

The ambulance companies sent about one third of their personnel to act as litter bearers with the infantry. CH went both as medic and interpreter.

As the hour approached, with the infantry lying tense along the jumping off line, and the gunners ready and waiting for their watches to tick the second when all should fire with one great crash. Suddenly a red rocket darted from the enemy's front line and brought down a barrage from the German guns!!! This lasted only a few minutes, but it took its toll of casualties from the devoted infantry. So well disciplined was the Division, that not a shot was sent in reply, and silence again fell over the entire field. CH and the other medics ran from soldier to soldier, as silently and out of view as possible, but still taking crazy risks to get the wounded moved back out of the way. "Thank you Jesus," thought CH as he got back to his position, just as the last seconds ticked off his watch.

CHAPTER 8

4:35 A.M. While it was still dark, there came an ear numbing roar. The clouds burst into red and yellow fire, the artillery barrage dropped with ground shaking booms just where it was expected to fall in the enemy line. The Infantry, who for so many months had survived gas and shells and bullets in the trenches of Lorraine and Picardy, rose like a great avenging storm and advanced according to plan. The assault traveled at the rate of one hundred meters in two minutes, the infantry followed close behind. CH's heart was pumping so hard as he ran, that he thought it might burst out and jump ahead. There were no trenches in which to find shelter! No place to hide. This was a different type of battle than he was used to. The broken nature of the ground made it hard to run and fire at the same time, still, he did it.

The enemy's artillery had not yet been accurately located, so they were still firing with deadly results. The advancing infantry suffered casualties from the beginning, but nothing daunted them. In the exhilaration of battle, they forgot their fatigue and the danger and ran resolutely in the wake of the bursting shells of their own guns. Soon prisoners were taken and moved to the rear. CH helped escort them back over the battleground, with bullets still flying by them. Several of the Germans had been wounded, some had to be carried. CH dressed their injuries as best as he could, and promised better care at the aid station.

At 5:30 the objective, Cravancon Farm, (about 2 kilometers from the jumping off place) was reached on schedule and everyone was buoyed by the success.

The line then advanced toward the second objective, the Missy-aux-Bois ravine, and on the way overran enemy batteries capturing or killing most of the gunners. The rest continued to fire until the Americans were among them. It was not an easy advance, there were heavy casualties on both sides. The enemy was dug deep and determined to defend the ravine.

Meanwhile, CH and the other soldiers escorted the prisoners to the dressing station. They were checked by medics and sent on to a prison camp. CH loaded his pack with medical supplies, something told him to take an extra gas mask, so he asked for one, and got it. CH left with the other soldiers to hurry back to join their battalion. It was not afternoon and he figured it would take two to three hours to catch up.

They reached the jumping off place without incident, but they knew from that point on it would be like 'no man's land.' They stayed there a few minutes to decide the safest way to go forward. There was a stand of bombed out trees and a small muddy ravine off to the right. It was still smoldering and smelled bad, probably from the bodies. Most of the men thought that was the way to go. It was out of the way by a quarter kilometer but they felt it was worth the time. They could still make it before dark. With that settled they picked up their packs and headed for the trees. As they made their way through the trees they picked up any usable guns, ammunition, and gas masks. CH suggested they cover their noses to protect from the smell and the lingering mustard gas. The sound of gunfire in the distance was getting closer. They were out of the trees now and the ravine was not giving them much cover.

They had not found anyone alive on the battlefield as yet, but they knew as close as they were, it could be anytime. CH said it was his duty to stop and help any wounded if he could. He was the only medic in the group. A corporal named Jerry said they had to keep going to reach their battalion before dark. CH had been given corporal status at Contigny, but said nothing. He picked up his pack load of guns and gas masks and walked on with the group, but stayed to the rear.

The small group of soldiers passed by the first objective, Cravancon Farm, and met with another group of prisoners being moved. They got directions to find their company, and headed on.

By twilight the gunfire was deafening. As the soldiers got closer to the battle, they could see the clouds of heavy mortar fire as they howitzers, machine guns and flame throwers were going at it. "Boys, I think we made it!" shouted Jerry. As he turned to look at the group, he noticed one missing. At that instant, a bomb fell out of the sky and wiped out the whole bunch!

CHAPTER 9

About 20 minutes after they had encountered the other group of soldiers with the prisoners, CH thought he heard someone call for help in English. He tapped the soldier in front of him, "Did you hear that?" "Yeah, I heard something. Sounded like an animal in pain or something like that.: replied the soldier. "I thought it sounded like someone calling for help," said CH. "Well, it coulda been that, but the corporal doesn't want to stop...." "Listen, I'm just going to make a quick check and I'll catch up with you in a few minutes." And off CH ran, in the direction of the sound.

Still wearing his gas mask, he made his way through the area where the cry had come from. He saw nothing, but lifeless bodies, both human and animal. Maybe it was just a sheep, or a dog. Wait...., there it is again! "Help!" In English. CH followed the voice, and saw a moving figure about30 yards away. As he approached the soldier, he saw that he was German. Cautiously, CH looked him over. The soldier had a gas mask and a gun, but was not holding it in firing position. CH could see both hands. The man was not a threat, so CH lowered his weapon. "Where are you hurt?" he asked in English. The soldier looked startled and said in German, "I do not speak English. I only know 'help' from hearing it from the other soldiers. I said it in German for awhile, and then in English for awhile. I was going to say it until my voice gave out, or somebody came to either help me, or kill me." CH then repeated, "Where are you hurt?" in German, as he knelt down beside the soldier, who was obviously in pain, but coherent.

He showed his wounds to CH, "I'm shot here and here." As CH cleaned and dressed the wounds, he noticed the burns on the man's body. His clothes were in shreds. "I'm surprised you can speak at all, with the gas still lingering," said CH. "I crawled around and took the gas masks from the dead until I got too weak. I'm almost blind, almost deaf, and it's getting hard to breath. I guess I'm dying," the German soldier replied. "Well, I'll try to get you some help. I don't know which station is closer, or easier to get to," said CH, as he looked at the darkening sky. "If we can get to that farm over the hill....look to the west, do you see what's left of a windmill?" asked the German soldier. "Yes, I see it," said CH. "Get me there, then you'll see a farm, not much of it left, but I can get help there," said the German soldier. "Okay, but I need to get some clean clothes on you, or your burns will get worse," said CH, as he pulled a coat off the body of a German soldier, and put it on the sounded soldier. Then CH took the coat off another dead German soldier, and put it on himself, as he grabbed a couple of good gas masks and ran back to get the wounded soldier.

Getting the soldier to his feet was really hard. His body was so weak, that he was dead weight. CH slung him over his shoulders, and started toward the windmill. It was slow going, and the lingering gas was affecting CH more than he realized.

CH found out that the soldier's name was Otto Schmidt, and he was a blacksmith before the war. His dream was to go to the "Big Kentucky Horse Race, in the USA" some day.

It was dark by the time they reached the windmill. CH was exhausted, and Otto was unconscious. "I've got to keep going, I just got to." "At least it's mostly downhill" thought CH, as he stumbled on.

When he reached what had probably been the house, there was only a doorway, with a door swinging back and forth, softly in the night. "Well, Otto, here we are at the farm," CH said in German to the unconscious man. His weakened legs gave out and he found himself sitting on the ground, with Otto still across his shoulders.

CH did not remember what occurred after that. When he awoke, he was in a German field hospital, on a cot with a cloth over his eyes. There were poultices on his arms and legs. When he tried to move his arm to take the cloth off his face, he realized that his arms were tied down.

A voice next to him said in German, "he's awake, doctor." Then another voice, "Well soldier, you had quite a time of it. How do you feel?" "I – I'm not sure. Where am I, and what happened to Otto? I was carrying Otto....the farm....?" "Oh oh yes, you and Otto, yes. Otto is recovering. He almost didn't make it. The gas has taken its toll on him. He will need to be cared for the rest of his life, unfortunately. He has five children, and at least he will be alive as they grow up."

"Now about you CH, Otto told us how you saved his life. He said you bandaged his wounds, got clothes for the two of you for protection, then you carried him on your shoulders nearly three kilometers to the pickup place. That's where our ambulance crew found you. You were unconscious, and holding Otto on your shoulders. You are a hero." Then the doctor explained that the restraints were just to keep him from hurting himself while he was unconscious, and now could be removed. They wanted him to rest, and then take some liquids. In a few days, he would be good as new. No permanent damage that they could find.

 CH was trying to figure out how this happened. Somehow, he is in a German hospital, and he isn't a prisoner?. They must think he is a German soldier. Did Otto know. Where are his dog tags? How long has he been here? More importantly, where is here? AND HOW IN THE HELL IS HE GOING TO GET OUT!!!!!

CHAPTER 10

After a few minutes of mentally trying to calm himself and collect his thoughts, CH reasoned that it could be worse, but he didn't want to go that direction again. "Okay", he thought, "they know my name, at least my first name, they don't seem to be treating me as a prisoner, my clothes are missing, my dog tags – missing, my boots – missing. I need to ask about that....and Otto. I need to talk to Otto. I've got to find out what he knows....and I need to find out how far behind the German lines we are....whoa boy, my eyes hurt!" CH pressed the medicated cloth into his eyes. It helped only a little. Someone came to bring a fresh dressing, and left again. CH figured since it was so quiet, it must be night. With his eyes swollen shut and hurting, he might as well try to sleep.

The next morning, CH awoke to someone gently lifting his head and putting a pillow under it, saying in German, "Good morning soldier. I have some tea for you".

- CH nodded a throaty "Thank you".
- "You are doing quite well for as long as you were exposed. The doctor says it's a miracle you and Schmidt survived at all."
- "Yeah, Otto got it full blast. I was at the other end, but it drifted over our way. After it was over, I was kind of confused and then I found Otto and you know the rest."
- "Yes, Otto has told us all how you carried him to the pickup place. You sure don't look like you are that strong to me."
- "Well, I have three brothers and I play the piano", said CH with a smile.
- "Yes, I guess you would have to be able to defend yourself. So I guess I believe you", replied the aide, smiling too. He held the cup of tea mixture for CH to sip, which he did, expecting tea. It was not.
- "What is this?" CH gasped nearly gagging, as he swallowed.

- "Oh, it's just a concoction of stuff that heals your throat really fast. I don't know exactly what's in it. The doctors call it 'tea'. Funny, huh? I don't think there is any tea in it."
- "How much of this 'tea' do I have to drink?"

- "A cup every three hours today. You'll get some soup too. At least you can talk and swallow. A lot of gas cases can't do either."
- "Listen do you know what happened to my stuff, or did I have anything when they picked up Otto and me?"
- "I don't know. I can check for you. I know you didn't have dog tags on when you came in."
- "Thanks. I've got a Luger that I really cherish, and I sure don't want to lose it. My father gave it to me when I went off to war."
- "Yeah, I sure understand. That would mean a lot. I'll go check right now and come right back. By the way my name is Clifford," and he hurried off.

Twenty minutes or so later, Clifford came back with a bag tagged "CH" on it, and knelt beside CH's cot. "I got it. I didn't look in it, but it feels like your gun is in there. Do you want me to open it and make sure?"

- "Can I take off the bandages for a few minutes so I can see too?"
- "Okay, I'll just slide it up a little so you can see, **IF** you can see."

Clifford pushed the bandage up above CH's eyebrows, and CH could barely peer out through his swollen, red, crusty eyelids, but he could see! He told Clifford to open the bag. He carefully removed the Luger, still in its holster with the belt. Someone had carefully wrapped it in a towel soaked in cosmolene, and some other oils to counter the damage from the gas. There were a few other pieces of personal stuff also wrapped carefully. Luckily, nothing that would arouse suspicion. He sighed in relief. CH asked if he could keep the bag with him, but Clifford said "No, but when he could see better and all the bandages were off, he could have his stuff." They would keep it locked up, so no one would steal it. CH agreed that he was pretty helpless at the moment.

Okay, now CH knows that the Germans think he is one of them. He knows what stuff he has left. He knows he came without dog tags. If he needs a number, he can use the same one he used the first time he infiltrated their trenches.

Now he needs a plan. He needs to know how far from the pick up place they are. If it's feasible, he should try to get back there. He ought to be able to get back to his lines from there. He has to find his company so someone can recognize him, after all, he doesn't have his I.D. And will be in a German uniform.

CHAPTER 11

This has to be just an aid station, thought CH, from what he could see when Clifford raised his eye dressing. The station may be moving to another position soon. He will have to find out when they will pull out, and hope he is able to disappear during the packing and tearing down. At least he hoped there would be a moment when no one would be looking. It's not much of a plan, but it's the only one CH could think of.

CH drank his tea. A little later, they brought him a thin broth. He survived this way for what he thought was another full day and night. His eyes were getting better, but his dressing continued to be bandaged. Clifford came by at least twice during his shift. CH got a little more information each time. Otto will be moved to a hospital in Germany. The aid station will be moved to a location closer to the battle field. Some of the patients will be sent back to the war. CH would be sent back to the war, most likely. Exactly when this would occur, Clifford didn't know. His best guess was in about 5 days, but it could be sooner. The Front needs all the medical personnel as soon as possible.

CH asked Clifford, "is there any way I will be able to see Otto before they ship him off to the hospital? Since I'm going back to the Front, I may never get a chance to see him again."

"I think so," replied Clifford, "Otto has been asking for you constantly. The doctor said he wished Otto had lost his voice instead of his sight. As soon as you can move around, we can walk over to see him."

"Clifford, help me up, see if I can stand!"

"You wake up right now?" Clifford thought for a few seconds, then took off the dressings from CH's eyes and helped him sit up with his feet on the floor. "I think I'm okay," said CH. "I don't feel too awful….but, I think I'd better sit here for a minute before I stand up."

"Your eyes look real good, how do they feel"

"Actually, they feel like I've got a horrible hangover. All blurry and sore, but I can see okay."

"That's good, you look pretty good for what you've been through. This may work out. Are you ready to stand now?"

CH nodded and positioned his feet. Clifford slipped his hands CH's arms and pulled him up. He held him and asked, "Do you want me to let go?"

"Let me shift my feet a little first……Alright, one arm at a time."

Carefully, Clifford let go of CH's arms, until he was standing alone, shaking all over but standing. He lasted about 4 ½ minutes. Then Clifford sat him down.

"Okay, if you practice sitting up as much as you can for the rest of the day. I'll come by and help you stand. Tomorrow, we will try walking a few steps. Maybe we should try crutches, but, they want you to go back to the war, so we need to get your strength up."

Within the day CH was taking steps with the help of a crutch. Feeling so much better, he said he wanted to see Otto. The doctor, pleased with CH's progress, felt it would be good for both of them to see each other.

About an hour after eating semi-solid food, CH, dressed in German pants and shirt, went to see Otto with Clifford by his side. On the way to Otto's bed, CH casually asked Clifford questions about himself. He seemed like a friendly, honest person. He was a few inches shorter than CH's 6 feet. But, he was just as skinny. He looked to be about 19-20 years old. "Well," said Clifford, "It's not much of a story. I was working on our farm with my parents and older brothers, when the war started back in 1914. My brothers went, but I was too young."

"My brothers have not been heard from since Verdun. My folks sent me to see if I could find them. Now I am a soldier except I have no stomach for killing. So, I was sent here to carry wounded and just help where I can. The doctors do not make me do too much because they think I am slow in the head. I am not as dumb as they think….don't let on about it. I'm still alive and I can search for my brothers. But I am afraid they might be dead."

"I'd say that is quite a story. Your searching for your brothers. Have you had any luck?" asked CH.

"I got some letters that they wrote, but didn't get mailed, from one of their friends. If it is true, they may still be alive. I'm hoping so, but it's not likely."

The two reached the other building and became silent as they went in. People were moving around inside doing their various jabs. A doctor asked what they wanted, and when Clifford mentioned CH, they doctor took them directly to Otto's bed.

Otto, who had been a stocky man, now resembled a starving moose. He was lying on a cot, covered with bandages from head to toe. "Schmidt," said the doctor, "Your 'CH' is here to see you."

"CH! I was afraid I would not see you again until after the war. They are sending me home, and you back to the Front. Tough luck, my friend." Said Otto in a raspy voice.

"Yeah, well, I wasn't as bad off as you." replied CH. Next time I rescue you, I hope you drop the weight before I hoist you on my shoulders."

"Ha ha ha! Chucked Otto, I guess I must look pretty bad, don't I"

"You do, what I can see of you, that is. You are bandaged all over."

CH sad how patched Otto's mouth was and reach over, picked up a cup of water, and held it to the man's lips saying, you look like you could use a drink." Otto sipped and swallowed the water hard." They haven't given me anything close to food yet. It's all been liquid so far. I'd sure like a beer right now though." replied Otto. Clifford was called away to help move a patient, said he would be back in a minute.

"Are we alone?" whispered Otto.

"Yes", whispered CH. "I have to tell you something important."

"It's okay to talk if we keep it low."

"It's about your dog tags."

"You know what happened to them?"

"Yes"

CHAPTER 12

Otto motioned for CH to come closer. CH put his ear close to Otto's face, and whispered softly "OK, tell me what happened."

– "I pulled them off your neck when you were carrying me to the pickup place. I dropped them somewhere close to the windmill, I think."

– "You became unconscious close to the windmill."

– "I dropped them before that. I remember doing it."

– "Why did you take them off?"

– "After you picked me up and started walking towards the windmill, I felt them and they were shaped wrong. I realized that you weren't a German soldier. I knew you would be in trouble if someone else saw them, so I pulled on them and they came off in my hand. I tried to avoid unconsciousness, but I felt it coming on. I dropped them before I blacked out. I have been worried since I woke up that you would be caught. No one else knows about you."

– "Thanks, Otto, I needed to know that."

– "Do you think you can get away?" I'll help you any way I can."

– "I think I can, maybe when they start moving everybody out. I should be able to slip out then. If I can get back to the pickup place, I'll be OK. I don't know how far we are from there."

– "Not far, about four or five kilometers, I think. It's all bombed fields. Nothing left."

– "What direction do I go from here?"

– "I'll think about it, I'm not sure, but I think there is a small creek just south of here. If you can get to it, follow it south and east, then...."

– "Shhh, someone's coming!" CH whispered just as Clifford came back

Clifford told Otto and CH that his shift was over, so he needed to get CH back to his bed. On the way back to the shed, Clifford said that the hospital would be moving in two days. They needed to hurry up and pack up and move everybody.

CH asked if he could see Otto again before they left. Clifford said he would try and get him to Otto the next day. He couldn't guarantee it, because they wanted to move the serious patients first and Otto was one of them. Then they would send the rest to the new location closer to the front lines. From there, CH and seven other soldiers would be released to go back to the war.

Clifford also told CH that the reason for the rush was that the Americans are pushing very hard and are very unpredictable in battle, so we need every soldier we have too go and fight them. Although Clifford had not personally seen one, he was told that the American soldiers are all huge and hard to do battle with. CH said that he had seen them and they are really big and aggressive. He hoped that he was physically well enough to go and fight such "gorilla-like" enemies. At least he was mentally ready to go back to the front and win this war.

CHAPTER 13

CH knew he had to be ready to disappear at any moment that the opportunity presented itself. He needed his stuff. It was still locked away. He also needed clothes and boots. So he asked Clifford if he could get a uniform.

"Yes," replied Clifford, "I will get one for you by tomorrow morning.:

"Can you get my personal stuff for me? I'll need to clean my luger and see how much damage there is. I might need a new holster for it."

Clifford agreed to get CH's stuff out and bring it to him right away. Which he did. He also brought some rags to clean it with.

CH spent the rest of the day cleaning the luger. The weapon was in good condition. The holster had protected it. The leather looked good but was brittle, even though it had been soaked in oil. Maybe he could find another one.

CH put his stuff inside his pillow slip and then laid on it. As he drifted off to sleep, he felt a calmness that he hadn't felt in weeks. This would all be over real soon. He thought, " Thank you, Lord."

The next morning CH was awakened by the hustle and bustle of cots being broken down, equipment being packed into bags. Loud voices and footsteps every which way. CH put his hand under his pillow to be sure his stuff was still there.

It was, he breathed a sigh of relief, and looked around. Everyone was busy getting ready to evacuate. He sat up on his cot to clear his head.

After a while, Clifford came in an obvious hurry, carrying a pile of clothes and boots.

"Here, CH, you need to put these on right away. I brought two pairs of boots. Keep whichever pair fits. They were in a pile we keep of patients' uniforms and boots. You'll probably get some different ones when we get to the next place."

CH stripped off the hospital gown and hurriedly got dressed in a German uniform that was almost a perfect fit. He stuffed his pockets with some of his stuff. When he tried to put his gun belt on, it cam apart in his hands. "Dammit," he thought, "I'll need another one."

Clifford, almost as if he could read CH's thoughts, "Let me go look for a belt. So the holster is bad too?"

"Yeah, it's pretty rotten, but I thought it would do." replied CH as he turned his attention to the boots. The socks and underwear had been washed and smelled of bleach. The first pair of boots looked the best but were too small. The second pair fit better but weren't in as good condition. "But, they were good enough," thought CH.

Clifford came back about then, carrying a back pack...and a really nice belt and holster for CH's luger. "This belonged to an officer.: Clifford explained. "It was in lock-up but the luger was gone. There was also some ammunition with it so you should be in good shape. You'll get a rifle when we get to the next place."

"Thanks, Clifford, you have been a great help---and a good friend." said CH. "I don't know what I'd have done without you."

"I was glad to do it, and I think of you as a friend, too."

"Do you have any idea where we are going?"

"No, they just said for us to be ready before 9 a.m."

"It's almost 9 now. I'd sure like to see Otto for a minute," said CH.

"OK, but they may have moved him out already. They are really in a hurry. Let's go find him!" CH put his knapsack on and so did Clifford.

They left the shed and hurried to where Otto might be. There were three horse-drawn ambulances waiting in line. They called out for Otto Schmidt, and got an answer from the last one.

"Here, here, I'm here" came the voice. They ran to the ambulance and climbed in. Otto was lying on the floor. "I'm sure glad to see you. I wasn't sure you'd come, they moved us so fast."

"Are you going to be all right, Otto?" said CH.

"Yes, they are sending me home." replied Otto. Clifford chimed in. "They are sending CH back to the front. I'm not sure he is physically strong enough. But I'm not a doctor."

There was a silence as the three men realized that they would never see each other again.

After a few minutes Otto pulled out a piece of paper and handed it to CH. "There is no way I can thank you for my life. My address is on that paper. If you make it through alive, come find me. My family will take care of you as long as you want to stay."

"Thanks Otto, I hope I can take you up an offer." After which, they shook hands, but Otto pulled CH close and hugged him. He whispered into CH's. "There is more than my address. I love you." He put his bandaged hands on CH's face for a few seconds, then dropped his hands. Noise from outside told them they must not linger. Clifford and CH said good-bye and climbed out of the ambulance. Clifford was near tears, so he kept his face down as they walked down the line of vehicles.

Then Clifford said something strange. "CH, I can get you to the windmill!"

"What do you mean—?"

"Otto told me about you, how you saved him even though you didn't have to. He said you are a good man, whatever country you are from. He told me you needed help getting back to the pick-up place and could I help. I promised I would help you anyway I could. And I will."

"Thanks Clifford, I can use your help, but, don't you have to go with the medical people? Won't they need you." "Not really, they think I'm slow and not too smart so they don't rely on me to do anything important. When they get this caravan going, they won't know exactly where I am, so I can slip out and hide till they get out of sight, which is pretty much what you were going to do, right?"

CH, surprised by Clifford's words, took a deep breath to compose himself and said: "You would do that for me?" "Yes, I would. We can slip out together. I know a good place to hide until they are out of sight."

CH and Clifford just laid low until the caravan started slowly towards the German lines. Suddenly two or three horses balked and all able-bodied men came to help calm them down. During the confusion, two figures disappeared. No one noticed anything. The horses were calmed and the caravan started again. CH watched as the last vehicle disappeared in the distance. It was muddy and slow moving but the caravan kept going.

"It will be dark by the time we get to the windmill, I brought enough food to keep us going for two or three days. I put extra in yours, because I know it will take awhile for you to find your division." "What are you going to do?" asked CH. "I'm going to look for my brothers. I know all this area, because I picked up wounded soldiers and took them to the 'hospital'."

So they agreed they would stay together until they reached the windmill. Clifford was going to backtrack to some of the villages and see if anyone knew of his brothers. CH was going back to where he thought his division was, and hoped they would recognize him.

CHAPTER 14

As they watched the caravan slowly disappear into the distance, a gentle mist began to fall, and wet their faces as they came out of their hiding place. Clifford pointed the way and said, "we are still behind German lines here, but the line has changed where the windmill is. I brought extra clothes for us to change into, so if we are caught by either side, we will look like civilians. I didn't have room for two pairs of boots, so we will lie and say we took the ones we are wearing off dead soldiers."

"Thanks Clifford. I'm glad you decided to come with me. I thought I was going to have to use Otto's map." replied CH. He pulled out a piece of paper that Otto had given him. "I drew the map. Otto asked me to do it. That is how I found out about your plan, I figured I might have a better chance of looking for my brothers if I went on my own." Clifford explained.

"But won't you be AWOL?" said CH.

"I don't know for sure, I never actually joined. I was given a uniform and told to go to either the hospital or the mess hall, and someone would show me what to do. I chose the hospital, because I could talk to the wounded soldiers and maybe learn something." replied Clifford.

"You've really thought this through. I think this is a good plan." said CH, as he hoisted his pack.

The two of them started walking. "You know, Clifford, I never have thought of you as slow." said CH.

"Thanks. It was just the way I had to act so that no one would expect too much of me. It's worked pretty well so far. I'll use it again, if we ever get caught." Clifford said.

"Let's hope that never happens. Since we are headed back to France, we may have to talk to someone, and I don't speak much French. I learned a few words, and I can understand some conversation, but...."

"It's all right, I speak enough French to keep us out of trouble. At least I hope I can." said Clifford.

"Well that's good to know." replied CH.

The two spent most of the day teaching each other what they knew about French. The way that Clifford was leading back to the windmill, they didn't encounter any people. There was an occasional small farm, but when they got close enough to see it well, it would be abandoned. They did find a chicken, and Clifford caught it after running around in circles as it squawked. He covered it with his blanket, and told CH that they would kill it and cook it when they got to the windmill. He said there was an underground bunker, and they could spend the night, or at least rest. He could see that CH did not yet have all his strength back, and was near exhaustion.

"Clifford, I'm not sure that I can go more than another mile or two. How much farther is it?"

"It's about another three hours, but we can stop at the next farm if you need to rest. There's not much daylight left, but I think I can find the windmill in the dark."

That sounds goo to me." said CH.

So, they headed toward a charred building, with a small pond near it. Clifford felt the burnt wood that had been the framework of a barn, to see if he could tell how long ago it had been burnt. It was cold to his touch. They crawled as far as they could into the barn where the beams provided some shelter, and dug a hole deep enough to keep themselves out of sight.

Clifford told CH to make a place to sleep, and he would go ahead and cook the chicken. Clifford made a small fire, and as the smoldering coals slowly baked the chicken, CH fell asleep. Clifford kept watch, and poked the bird occasionally to see if it was done. "Ah-h-h-h, perfection, if I do say so myself."

Suddenly, a sound came from another part of the barn. Clifford quietly woke CH, "SOMEONE'S IN HERE", he whispered. "Get your gun out." CH got his weapon and put the clip in, then laid low, waiting to be attacked. Their hearts were beating so fast, they were sure that whoever it was would hear.

"Show yourselves!" said CH in his best German soldier voice. A few seconds later, a small voice, shaking with fear, spoke in French, "Please sir, we are hungry." A smaller voice was whimpering nearby. Clifford stood up to see two young children, dirty from head to toe, tears rolling down their cheeks.

"Are you alone?" he queried in French.

"Yes sir, it's just me and my brother."

"Then come over here, now!" commanded Clifford. The children came, holding on to each other tightly. Clifford pulled a leg off the chicken, and handed it to them. He then lifted them down into the hole and handed them the other leg of chicken, which they nearly swallowed whole.

For almost an hour, they all ate until the chicken was just a small pile of bones. They also had bread and cheese, which Clifford took out of his knap-sack. CH motioned for them to lay by the smoldering embers, and then covered them with his blanket. Clifford said CH needed more sleep too, so he would keep watch. Two or three hours went by. Clifford woke CH to take over the watch. The children were sound asleep. A full tummy and a warm place to sleep were just what they needed. CH and Clifford decided to stay there all night. They took turns keeping watch, while the other slept. In the morning, they would discuss what to do next.

CHAPTER 15

Morning came with a blaze of sunlight making its way through the charred building that once housed cows and other farm animals. They were long gone, but the aroma hung in the air.

The campfire was almost completely out. Clifford had the last watch, so that CH could be rested for the next leg of their journey. Clifford had made enough coffee for the two of them. He had found an old water pump that still worked, filled their canteens, and brought a bucket of fresh water back.

As soon as CH smelled the coffee, he awoke. "That smells good." he said, in a soft voice. So he wouldn't wake the children. As they sipped the strong black German coffee, they whispered softly to each other about their new "situation", and what they should do about it.

"We can't leave them here, they'll starve to death." said CH matter-of-factly.

"No, we will have to take them with us even though it will slow us down some. I'm sure glad I packed extra food. Maybe, if we're lucky, we will find another chicken." replied Clifford.

"That would be great." said CH, just as the two children began stretching themselves awake. They finished their coffee and began repacking their knapsacks, each leaving out a little piece of the hard rye bread and cheese, so the children could eat.

CH smiled as he gave the food to the two young boys. "Do you speak German?" he asked. The older boy said he could a little, and indicated with his fingers how little. So Clifford took over in his weak French. "I know a little French." as he indicated with his fingers.

"And I know even less," said CH, as he indicated with his fingers. They all laughed, even the youngest boy, who had been so frightened the night before.

"My name is Clifford, what's yours?"

"Claude, and I am seven. My brother's name is Henry, and he is four." The little one held up four fingers.

"Henry is my father's name," said CH.

"Claude is my uncle's name," replied Clifford. Then Clifford poured some water on what was left of the fire and washed his hands and face in what was left in the bucket. Ch did the same, and offered it to the boys. They followed what Clifford and CH did, even though they were dirty from head to toe.

"We'll get cleaned up later," said Clifford. "Right now we need to get going. Do you boys know this area? Was this your home?"

"This was Grandfather's farm. Our mother and father left us here and went away. Then the soldiers came and burned everything. Grandfather put us in the barn and told us to stay here and not to look out. The soldiers did not know about us. They took Grandfather away, then they burned down the barn. We ran and hid in the pond 'til they left. As soon as we could, we went back in the barn where we had been. There was some food there."

"Is there any food left? Show us where you were." said Clifford excitedly. They boys climbed through the burnt barn timbers to what looked like a hole in the floor, with a makeshift door. When Clifford moved it, he could see it was a cold storage room, with baskets in it, but they were all empty.

"We ate the potatoes and onions, but when they were all gone, we were too afraid to come out." explained Claude.

"How long were you here without food?" asked Clifford.

"Three, maybe four days. Our tummies hurt so much, then we smelled the chicken, and....and."

"It's alright," said CH. ,"You did the right thing."

"We were glad to share our food with you." replied Clifford, as he searched for edible food. He shook out feed bags and felt along the walls to see if there was anything at all. It was so low that he had to crawl around. Then he felt what seemed to be a box, which he dragged out into the daylight, and forced it open. Amazingly, the contents were clean and dry. Straw was packed around a bag of rye flour, two small bags of sausages and three containers of water, matches and a small lantern.

"Your Grandfather must have put this here in case he and you boys might have to hide for awhile. Thanks to him, we have enough food to last us all for some time. I'll use these feed bags to put the food in. CH and I will carry the heavy stuff. We'll use the other feed bags as knapsacks for each of you boys."

Some of the bags were made of canvas, so those became the knapsacks, and were filled with what the boys would need. Claude carried Henry's knapsack, and the four of them started off in the direction of the windmill.

CHAPTER 16

As the four walked toward the windmill, they talked and learned more of each other's language. After about an hour or two, Henri` began to cry. CH asked, "What's wrong?" And Claude said,"He's getting tired, and so am I."

"Well," said CH, "I think I could do with a little rest myself."

"I agree. Let's find some shade. The sun is very warm today." replied Clifford, as he handed his extra pack over to CH. Then he reached down and lifted Henri`, and put him on his shoulders. They began walking again, looking for shade.

After a little while, they were at the crest of a small hill. Claude saw a small grove of trees just a little way away. As they quickened their step, CH noticed that little Henri` was sound asleep. He thought of Otto, and how he carried him across his shoulders. He had been much stronger then. The mustard gas had really taken a toll on him. He prayed a silent prayer that they would all get to the windmill in good shape.

They finally reached the grove of trees. For whatever reason, the trees were in good shape. Apparently, they were not in the path of the war. CH wondered if they were still behind German lines, and exactly where the lines were.

Ch put his stuff down, and gently lifted Henri` off Clifford's shoulders, and laid him down in the cool grass. Claude cradled his little brother's head in his lap. They all laid on the ground, and it felt so good that they all did a collective sigh. Claude soon fell asleep. CH dozed, and Clifford rested, but still kept his eyes and ears open.

After a little while, Clifford did some rearranging of the packs, to make them easier to carry. CH opened his eyes and saw what Clifford was doing, and began helping.

"While I was dozing, I thought, or dreamed, that I smelled something sweet like pears or peaches. Do you smell it?" queried CH. Clifford put his nose up and took a deep breath. "Yes, I smell it now." So they looked around up in the trees. "Look!" There's a cherry tree over there! You stay here with the boys, and I'll go get some." exclaimed Clifford.

He picked cherries until he couldn't reach any more. He took his shirt off, and piled it full. Then he carried his treasure back to the others. The boys were awake now, so Claude climbed the tree and picked more cherries. Clifford pulled a piece of feed bag out and put all the cherries in it. They had picked about four or five quarts, Clifford surmised.

Then he and CH decided it was time to get going. CH said he had an idea. He looked around and found two limbs on the ground, small enough in diameter to become poles. He took his knife and trimmed off the branches, then he asked Clifford for one of the larger heavier feed bags. Clifford emptied out one and gave it to CH. CH took the cord that was on the feed bag, and tied it to the two poles.

By this time, Clifford knew what CH was making and pulled the cords from the other feed bags. They tied them to the poles, and made a sturdy litter. They put as much of their bags of food, etc. on the litter, as they could. CH took one end and Clifford took the other, and together they lifted it. It was not as heavy as a man, or even the older boy, so the little group started out for the windmill again. This time, neither of the boys had to carry anything. Since it was easier walking, they made good time.

It was late afternoon when they saw the windmill. They boys wanted to run to it, but Clifford told them to wait. He and CH put down the litter, and Clifford walked carefully to the windmill. It was empty. He looked inside for the bunker. It was in good shape, except for the spiders. "I hate spiders." he said to himself, as he checked everything out. Then he went back and got the others. They decided to spend the night and talk about what they should do.

The bunker was a little larger than the root cellar had been. It was probably a hiding place for the German soldiers for awhile. The windmill had been totaled by the fighting, but the bunker had been dug out far under ground, and was not visible in any way. You had to know it was there.

There were mess kits and utensils, and a makeshift stove, with a small pipe going up to the outside, where smoke would dissipate into the brush and disappear.

After they unloaded the litter, they hid it from sight, and went down into the bunker. "Whew," said CH, "it smells like the trenches."

"Well, it's home for tonight." said Clifford.

It was cool and dry as they made places to sleep. Clifford cleaned out the mess kits as well as he could and put cherries in them, added some of the rye flour, and smashed it all together. Then he made a small fire and put them on the grate of the stove to bake.

They ate sausage and cheese, with the cherry stuff for dessert. "It actually tastes pretty good." remarked CH. "I didn't know you could cook." "Yes, I can do a lot of things when I have to." said Clifford. The boys seemed to like it too. They ate every bit of it.

CH and Clifford put the boys to bed close to the stove, and bedded down next to them until they fell asleep, which took all of about five minutes. Clifford motioned for CH to follow him just to out of earshot of the boys. "Well, we need to talk." Clifford said softly. "I know," CH said – almost sadly, "but we knew this was where we would part company."

The two men spent the next hour or so making plans for the coming day, then they bedded down for a good night's rest.

CHAPTER 17

Morning came and they all woke up to the smell of coffee and toast. Clifford had made the coffee and sliced a few thin slices of bread, and laid it near the glowing embers. He mashed some of the cherries, and made a jelly-like substance, heaped it on the toast and handed one to each of the others, keeping one for himself.

They ate every bite as though a French chef had cooked a feast. Then the little band of travelers packed up their belongings, and added whatever they could find that might be needed....there wasn't much....the Germans had been thorough when they vacated. CH went up the steps to the outside. His eyes took awhile to adjust to the sunny sky. He saw no one and heard nothing, so he continued until he was out of the bunker, then signaled Clifford that it was safe, so he could bring the supplies, and the boys. Claude and Henri skipped up the steps and into the sunlight. They were in a playful mood, and neede to have a little fun before they began their march.

They decided to have a treasure hunt. Claude was the first to find something, a rusty belt buckle. Henri found a cracked mirror, so they were even. Meanwhile, CH and Clifford packed the litter and put their knapsacks on.

The night before, when they were talking, Clifford had remembered a farm just two kilometers due south of the windmill. It had not been burned to the ground like so many were. CH said that he thought that the farm was probably in Allied hands now. Clifford agreed. According to his rough map, and information he had gotten from some of the patients, all the land south of Belleau Wood was now under American and Allied control.

CH was glad for the news, and told Clifford that would be the best way to go, since the way he had gotten to the windmill was through battlefields. The mustard gas lingers a long time and he wouldn't want to go that way.

So they gathered up the litter and called to the boys to come to them. Claude and Henri had a whole handful of "treasures", which they put in their pockets, and ran back to the men. Off they all went.

The weather was very warm this time of year in France, and CH and Clifford were soon sweating. They kept the pace a little slower so the boys wouldn't fall behind. The way to the farm was pretty much uneventful. They stopped twice to rest their hands and the boys had to potty.

They were within a few hundred yards of the farm, when CH said he saw movement there. He couldn't tell if they had on uniforms or not. Clifford said he would go investigate, so CH found a tree and some bushes where he and the boys could be out of sight.

CHAPTER 18

Clifford left his knapsack with CH, and walked right up to the fence of the farm, unlatched the gate, and went to the door and knocked. No answer. He then knocked harder and called out in French, "is anybody there?" He heard a noise inside and then a voice called out, "who's there?"

- "My name is Clifford. I'm looking for my two brothers, can you help me?"
- "Wait there for a minute."
- Four or Five minutes later, an older man opened the door a crack. "Are you alone?" he said tentatively.
- "No, I have two little boys and another man. They are waiting to see if it's OK to come."
- "How old are the boys?"
- "Seven and four. I'm 18 and the other man is twenty-something." said Clifford, then he added, "We are really tired and hungry."
- A woman's voice said "Go and get them, and bring them here. We have some food, not much, but we will share."

Clifford excitedly waved for CH and the boys to come. The door was opened and all were welcomed in, especially Claude and Henri. Clifford tried to explain about how he and CH had found the two young boys, then he let them tell the story of their parents and grandfather.

By this time, the woman, whose name was Mimi, had put some bread, cheese, and fresh fruit on her table, and told them to all sit down, which they were glad to do. CH tried out his French, and they all laughed. Then Claude and Henri took their "treasures" out of their pockets, and laid them on the table for everyone to see.

Mimi seemed to take a special liking to the boys, so she started separating the treasures and remarking on each object. Something caught CH's eye and he asked if he could look closer. He picked it up and rubbed it on his shirt to clean it, and nearly jumped for joy. "Whee hoo!" he shouted. "It's my dog tag. Where on earth did you find it?" Henri said he found it near the windmill. He wasn't sure what it was, but if it was CH's then he should keep it.

CH thanked him and said "You are quite the treasure hunter, Henri." Henri beamed at that. "This changes a lot of things. I can get my identity back." Mimi asked, "Are you really a soldier? Which army are you? Your French is not so good."

- "Please don't be afraid, I'm an American."
- "You are an American?" she said in English. "You are a Hero!" she shouted this time in French, as she jumped up and hugged him.
- "Thank you for saying that, but I'm only one soldier, and I need help getting back to the front lines."
- Clifford was taking all this in, then he asked CH, "You sort of lied to me back at the hospital, didn't you? But I am glad you are not a German soldier."
- "I didn't tell you the truth then, because I didn't know you yet. I was going to tell you before we parted ways. You are my friend, and I didn't mean to mislead you."
- Clifford saw how sincere CH was, and said "It is all right. You are still my friend."

Mimi's husband interrupted by saying he had a map from the Americans, and it might help CH and Clifford get to wherever they needed to go. He got the map and gave it to CH, who thanked him and looked at it with Clifford. It showed they were in American-held territory. The Germans were being pushed back. Some of the people were going back to their homes, at least the ones that had homes left to go to.

CHAPTER 19

As Clifford looked over the map, Mimi's husband, Jean Pierre, showed them where they were. A small "X" marked the farm. Jean Pierre told them the direction they needed to go in order to get to the road the Americans were using to move men, horses, and guns to the front. There were some railway tracks and he told them to follow the tracks. That would take them to Chateau-Thierry, where they would start seeing soldiers, who could direct them to the field headquarters.

Clifford said he knew that was the direction CH needed to travel. It would be a long day's walk to get there. Clifford said he and the boys would go some of the distance with CH, and then they would part ways. Mimi interrupted and said "No, it is too dangerous for the boys". She had a better idea. She knew that CH needed to get back to his unit, but Clifford, Claude and Henri could stay at the farm for awhile, helping the elderly couple repair the fence and barn.

Mimi had been keeping a secret all day. Now she would share it. She and her husband had been given a ride to their farm the last time they were in town. They had two horses and a cow tied to the back of the horse-drawn cart. They had quickly hidden their animals in the barn, when they heard the knock at the door. Ch could ride one of the horses to Chateau-Thierry, go to the blacksmith and leave the horse there. The blacksmith was a relative, and they would pick the horse up the next time they went to town again. Ch and Clifford liked Mimi's idea, so it was decided.

Clifford helped Jean Pierre saddle up the horse while CH said goodbye to the little boys. Tears rolled down Henri's face as CH picked him up and hugged him. Claude cried too, but was glad that he and his little brother had a place to stay. Clifford had tears in his eyes as he and CH said goodbye to each other.

"I hope you find your brothers, and I hope they are alive and well," said CH.. "I hope so too. Please look for me after the war is over. I pray you get through it all right," said Clifford softly, holding back his tears.

"Thank you, Clifford. Yes, I will try to find you, and Otto too, if I make it through. You have been a good friend and I will never forget you." "I don't mean to rush you, but if you want to get there today, you need to leave soon," said Jean Pierre. CH climbed on the horse. Mimi gave him a sack with some sandwiches and fruit. CH leaned down and kissed her on the cheek. "You have been so good to us. God bless you."

CH walked the horse at a slow pace to get used to him, all the while waving to everybody, as they were waving back. It was a sad moment, but CH needed to be on his way.

CHAPTER 20

CH trotted off in the direction of the railroad tracks, then turned around and trotted back to the little group. He stopped and, looking very sheepish, said, "It might be a good idea if I knew this horse's name." In response to which, it sent everyone into a laughing fit. Even the horse got into the act by stomping the ground, nodding his head and neighing loudly.

John Pierre, trying to compose himself, said " Marcel, his name is Marcel, and if he wonders off you need to call him by whistling like this: Thhh-ooo-eee-oh Marcel! He knows his whistle." So all of them put their mouths in the position Jean Pierre had just shown them and repeated "Thhh-ooo-eee-oh Marcel!" and then they all laughed again. "Thank you very much" grinned CH as he turned Marcel around and started off again, listening to the little boys whistling behind him. This time, leaving was not so sad.

CH was not an experienced horseman, but he knew how to ride. After a couple of hours trotting at an easy pace, his behind was going numb, so he decided to stop and rest. He tied the horse to a small tree, and sat down to open his pack. He brought out an apple, which he promptly gave to Marcel, patting him on the neck. "I'll get us some water," as he took one of his two canteens, poured some of it into his mess kit, and held it so the horse could drink. CH took two swigs, and put the lid back on the canteen. "That's about all we can have for now," as he buckled up his backpack. Then he sat down and looked at the map. According to it, he was about two or three hours away from Chateau-Thierry. He looked at his watch, it was 4:30 PM. He would be there well before dark. "Good", he thought, "I should be able to have time to look for the blacksmith, then get some bearing on where the Americans were quartered.

CH walked for about a half an hour, holding Marcel's reins, and the horse walked contentedly behind. After his rear end and legs felt better, CH got back on the horse. He trotted Marcel and kept near the railroad tracks.

It was pretty much an uneventful journey. He only saw one carriage and one automobile coming the other way, to which he smiled and waved and said "Good afternoon", in French, and trotted on.

By 6:30, he was at the outskirts of the town. "Hmmm," he said to the horse, "I think it's not too far to the blacksmith's. We made it." CH smelled the air and listened for the sound of an anvil, and turned his ride towards it.

The blacksmith spoke English better than CH spoke French, so they talked in English. After taking off the saddle, bridle and blanket, they rubbed down Marcel, and put him in a stall with fresh hay. "He's a good horse", said CH. "We got along very well."

"I'll keep him here until Jean Pierre comes for him." replied the blacksmith, who said his name was Lewis. CH gave his name and they shook hands. Then CH pulled out his map and the two studied it to see where CH needed to go to find the headquarters and Americans.

With the map in hand, the two men shook hands (actually forearms), then CH walked toward the headquarters.

CHAPTER 21

As CH made his way through the town, he passed many people. Since the battle of Chateau -Thierry had been long and bloody, the people were wanting to return to normal life. The liberation was glorious, and people wanted to come home.

It was early evening, and he was hungry. There were many wagons and tables filled with food to buy. CH went through his pockets to see how much money he had. Nothing. "Well," he thought, "I do have some of Mimi's sandwiches left, and some fruit. No, he had given the fruit to the horse." So CH walked along the street eating his sandwich. It tasted really good, but he was passing by some cafe's and the smells of French cooking was almost overwhelming to his senses.

He finished the sandwich, and was searching through his knapsack for something - anything else he could eat. He tripped over a rut and nearly fell. His gyrations of trying not to hit the ground did not go unnoticed. As he straightened up and looked around, hoping no-one saw him, he realized he had been seen. Several people sitting at the tables in an outdoor cafe looked at him, but not really laughing. Just smiles on their faces.

A young woman came over to him and asked if he needed to sit down for a moment. She took him by the hand and led him to a table where her family was sitting. A chair was pulled up and he sat down, still embarrassed.

An older man asked him in French if he was okay. CH nodded and said "Yes", in French. A glass of wine was placed in front of him. He put up his hand to indicate No, he had no money to pay.

The older man said "Drink, drink, it's on me." CH thanked him and nearly finished the wine in one gulp, sat the glass down and thanked him again. As he sat, everyone was trying to talk to him at once in French. "Whoa," he said throwing up his hands. "I only speak a little French. Does anyone speak English?" Two of the six people said "Yes". Ch was much relieved, and they all sat and talked for a little while.

As CH looked around the cafe, he noticed that inside was a piano. He asked if anyone played. The young woman said her grandfather played when he was alive, but he was killed during the fighting. That was some time ago. She said she was learning from her grandfather, but she was not good enough yet to play for the cafe.

CH asked if he could play to pay for his wine. "Oh yes," said the young woman, whose name was Yvette. As CH got up to go to the piano, everyone clapped for him. He laid his knapsack on the floor beside him as he sat down at the old piano.

His fingers caressed the keyboard, as he rolled them up and down to exercise them. People stopped talking, and listened. CH played a concerto by DeBussey, and brought some to their feet, and tears to the eyes of others. As he played on for awhile, more people crowded around and glasses of wine started to accumulate on the top of the piano. CH took a sip occasionally, but was so happy to be playing the piano, that he lost all track of time.

It was dark by the time he noticed, so he finished the piece he was playing, did some "finale rolls", and stopped, stood, and bowed to everyone. Clapping and cheering followed, then he took Yvette aside, and told her he needed to get to the AEF encampment. She said she couldn't take him, but her brother would. She went to the kitchen of the cafe and returned with a young man.

"This is Adrien, my brother. He speaks some English. He knows where the headquarters is for all the troops. They will help you find the right encampment. Are you a soldier?" she queried. "Yes, said CH. I am an American. I escaped the Germans several days ago. It's a long story. I'll tell your brother about it as we go, and he can tell you when he gets back. Thank you all for everything."

With tears rolling down her cheeks, Yvette reached up and kissed CH. "Thank you from all of us. The Americans saved us, and your piano playing reminded us of Grandfather, and happier days."

"I do have a favor to ask," said CH. "Do you know the Blacksmith, Louis?"

"Yes, he's the only one left."

"If it's not too much trouble, could you get a message to him about me? I need him to know that I got back to my unit." said CH.

"Oh yes, I can do that for you. I'll go early tomorrow."

"Thank you, he will pass it along to his relatives who helped me." said CH. "I hope I can see you again Yvette." He bent down and kissed her on the cheek.

Adrien came up in a small horse-drawn buggy. "This will get us there quickly. Climb in." CH climbed in next to Adrien, and they were off, amid the cheers and applause.

CHAPTER 22

As the lights of the town dimmed in the distance behind them, the path before them seemed dark and lonely. Only the moonlight drifting in and out of the trees lighted the night. The horse clippety-clopped in a steady rhythm to the wheels creaking as they rode silently into the night.

CH was the first to speak, "How far is the encampment?"

"About a half hour more," replied Adrien.

"Have you been there enough to know which one is the Americans'?"

"Yes, I drive a wagon load of food and supplies once or twice a week. I will take you to the right place, don't worry."

As they rode on, CH began telling Adrien the story about Otto, Clifford and the German field hospital. How they escaped, and found the boys. Finding Jean Pierres' farm and all their help.

Soon the lights of the encampments came into view. There were several soldiers standing around smoking cigarettes, and Adrien called out to them in French, "It's Adrien, from Chateau-Thierry."

"OK, you can pass. Did you bring anything for us?"

"I have cigarettes and some wine for the American General, but I have enough to give you some too."

Adrien handed a bottle of wine and cigarettes to the soldiers. "My sister rolled the cigarettes," he said.

"Thanks, we'll enjoy them."

Adrien drove on to the American Division, and stopped at the officers' tent. "I will give the cigarettes and wine to the general, and you can find out where your unit is," he said to CH.

"All right, thank you for helping me."

They got down from the wagon, and told the soldier on guard duty, who they were. He went inside to tell the general.

When he came back, he told them to go inside, which they did. Adrien handed the general the wine, and the general smiled as he looked at the wine bottles nestled in a wooden box. He opened one of the bottles, and poured some into a glass and two cups. He handed Adrien and CH the cups, apologizing that he only had one glass left. They sat and drank the wine as CH explained everything that had happened.

The general seemed amazed that CH had survived and was alive to tell about it. He then ordered his assistant to radio the medical unit that CH was part of. An audible "Well I'll be damned!" came from the other end of the radio. Soon CH's sergeant and two officers came running into the tent. "Engelbert!", he shouted in recognition. "Son, we thought you were dead."

"Well, here I am, with a real good tale to tell you. Where is the French Lieutenant?"

"I'm sorry, but he was killed a week ago. He was a good man."

Adrien excused himself. He needed to go back to town, but first there were some letters to be mailed. He collected them, and he and CH said their goodbyes.

The sergeant and the two officers explained to the general how important CH was to their unit, and how they missed all of his abilities.

"We'll get you a uniform in the morning. For tonight, we'll just talk and get a good night's sleep. Tomorrow, we'll put you to work. There are some German prisoners, so we need you to interpret for us," said the general. You showed up at a good time. We need your talents."

They all talked for awhile, then CH walked to his unit with his sergeant and the two officers. He was handed a bedroll, and they settled down for the night.

CH had so much going on in his head, that he couldn't sleep. He had a gut feeling that something really big was about to unfold.

CHAPTER 23

Daybreak found CH in a fresh uniform, drinking a cup of coffee and downing some French pastries as he headed to Division Headquarters. Once there, he was ushered inside to receive his orders. The general wasn't there yet, but had left instructions for him to wait, so he passed the time by looking at a huge map marked with circles, X's and arrows. CH saw the places he had been, and where the Allied war machine was. It was interesting to see how far back the Germans had been pushed. He knew it was at great cost. He bowed his head and said a silent prayer for those who were lost in the effort.

Soon, in came the general, with three officers behind him trying to keep up. CH stood at attention, saluting. The General waved a salute back and said "at ease" in one pass. He grabbed up a stack of papers and nearly yelled "You have to tell me what's in here. My German is terrible, and the only other interpreter is Moroccan. That guy speaks German and Arabic. No help there."

CH took the papers and began reading out loud, as the general's assistant began typing. After he was finished, the general called another headquarters, and began telling what was in the papers. Afterwards, he thanked CH, and told him to stick around for awhile. The phone rang and the general talked for about ten minutes. "We need the German officers brought in," he nearly shouted. "This is very important. Are you ready to interrogate these prisoners? General Pershing, and General Foch are deciding the next offensive."

"Yes Sir, I can do it. You just ask the questions, and I'll get the answers."

So the German officers were brought in, and allowed to sit at a table. The general began politely. CH spoke softly to the officers, which they were not expecting. They began answering the questions, and were very polite also.

After the general felt he had all the information he needed, he asked the prisoners if they were comfortable with their accommodations. They seemed surprised, but said everything was fine.

CH walked back to the compound with the prisoners, talking and carefully making sure what they told the general was accurate. He then walked back to the open tent where the general was looking at the map. The general motioned for CH to come over, and asked "Well, were their answers correct?"

"How did you know......?"

"I figured you would check up on them. It's what I would do. You <u>are good</u> at all of this."

"Thank you Sir. I knew you needed to be sure that you had accurate information."

"We are about to start another offensive." said the general. "I talked with General Pershing, and he would like for you to be with the 'Big Red 1' when they begin the battle. We are hoping this will go fast, and possibly end the war."

"Yes Sir, I would like to be there." replied CH. He thought to himself, "Wow, General Pershing wants me at the front with him!"

CHAPTER 24

CH, while thrilled that he would be with General Pershing, found himself apprehensive at going back into the war. "I hope I still have the guts to fire a gun at another human," he thought. "I am a doughboy, and I will do whatever I must, when the situation calls for it."

As CH pondered his abilities the Brigadier General called him over to the map. Pointing to different places, he explained where the Big Red 1 would be deployed. Exactly when the offensive would begin, was still being discussed. This would be charging into the Argonne Forest, and a lot of hand to hand combat, with only trees to hide behind. The enemy would also be behind trees. "We have pushed them back and it has been costly to the Allied Forces." "Yes sir, it was that way at Contigney. They kept coming, and we kept pushing them back." CH said.

"Yes, it will be very hard on us. I pray that we don't lose too many men, but this Division has been the leader in nearly every battle so far, and the Allied Command is counting on us. We have never let them down, and we won't start now. We are close to the end, and we will see it through." replied the Brigadier General, with pride in his voice.

The Brigadier General went on to say that he was waiting for more information, then they would be starting the march to the front. artillery divisions were already in place, and firing on the enemy. "You stay here and study the map. We will be leaving shortly."

CH began memorizing the map, and where they would be deployed. His company would be right up front, as usual. A few minutes later, the phone call came. Start the move!

The Brigadier General climbed into a truck, and CH climbed in behind him. There were several other officers already in the truck. CH was the only enlisted man. The ride was bumpy and uncomfortable, but it beat walking and carrying a heavy back pack.

CH watched the landscape as best he could, trying to imagine the map, and where they were. The Brig. General watched him. He could almost see CH's brain working.

After about an hour the Brig. General asked CH where they were, and CH told him. The Brig. General then asked the driver if that was correct. The driver said it was. "How do you do that?" asked the Brig. General. "You only had a few minutes to study the map."

"I have a good memory, sir." replied CH, "I have always been able to do it."

"Well doesn't that beat all. I think you have a photographic memory."

"Yes sir, I've been told that," said CH.

About then a plane flew over, and everybody near a window looked to see whose it was. "It's one of ours!" they shouted in unison. "We are getting close, I can hear the artillery fire." "Driver, how much farther?"

"We'll be at the meeting place in about 20 - 25 minutes, sir." replied the driver. Everyone stayed alert from that point on. Enemy fire might be able to reach that distance, and enemy planes could be lurking in the skies.

When they got to the meeting place, there was a variety of vehicles nestled under some trees. The Brig. General told the driver to find a place under the trees. He did, and they all got out. The Brig. General led the way to the center of the trucks, where they saw General Pershing talking to some of the other officers. He was giving a pep talk about the upcoming offensive. When the Brig. General and CH walked up, Gen. Pershing stopped talking, and motioned for the Brig. General and CH to come closer. Everybody saluted each other. Gen. Pershing said to the Brig. General, "I presume this is the soldier you told me about?" He then shook CH's hand and said, "The information you translated turned out to be extremely important to our offensive. I just had to meet you....except I feel that I have already met you. Perhaps a few months back, the French were giving out some battlefield awards. You were there weren't you?"

"Yes Sir."

"I don't forget faces, and yours stayed with me. You are an asset to our cause, and I wanted to tell you that in person."

"Thank you Sir. I'm glad I was of help."

Gen. Pershing shook CH's hand again, and said he hoped to see him after the war was won. Then Gen. Pershing turned his attention back to his speech to the Allied officers. After he finished speaking, he climbed into his vehicle, and the driver whisked him away.

CHAPTER 25

October 1-2, 1918 The command changed over to Division One at 4 A.M. The Infantry had moved into position behind a ridge that hid them from the enemy. They were dug in as best they could. Enemy fire was pelting the entire area.

It was decided that the new time for the offensive to officially start would be October 4 at 5:30 A.M.

The soldiers had to wait and not fire even though enemy artillery battered them constantly for three days. Our artillery fired back to keep the enemy from advancing. Mustard gas had been pumped into one area so thick, one company had to be removed and taken back to the nearest medical station.

CH sat with the Brigadier General for the 3 long days and nights, as German artillery fire fell all around them. Then it was H-hour and the offensive began. There were heavy casualties on both sides. Gains into the Argonne were hard fought. CH gave medical aid again and again, along with other medics and litter bearers.

One one run to help the wounded, CH heard the cry of an animal in pain. It was very close. He stepped over a dead German soldier and there it was...a dog lying under some debris. He pulled the debris away, and the dog, a German Shepherd, was almost completely covered in mud. He tried to get up, but couldn't. CH saw blood on the dog's hip. He knelt down and began talking to the dog in his pigeon French. "It's OK, boy, I'm here, let me get a good look at you." The dog whimpered but didn't attempt to bite. "So you are a German-German Shepherd. You're the first one I've seen." he said in German. He put sulfa powder on the wound, picked the dog up and made his way back to the medic station. Once there, he laid the dog on the ground and began working on him. Another medic camp up, saw CH with the dog. "What have we here? A dog!"

"Sh-h-h, yes, it's a dog," whispered CH. "He's been shot."

"I see" whispered the medic. "I can help if we hurry, there's no wounded humans right now." So the two of them fixed up the dog. They removed a bullet fragment that was lodged in his hip joint and stitched up his wound. He laid quietly as they worked on him. They bandaged his wound and covered him with an old blanket.

"He will be asleep in a few minutes, I gave him a sedative." said CH.

"Good, it will keep him quiet long enough for his wound to stabilize. "said the medic, whose name was Joe. I"I don't think anyone will see him back here."

"That's what I thought." replied CH.

Then the two of them went back to work. It didn't surprise CH that Joe helped with the dog. Joe was a really good guy, and had studied medicine back in the states. He wanted to be a surgeon.

CH finished his "shift" and took his bedroll and laid down near the dog. He was asleep in seconds, even though artillery fire filled the night.

When CH awoke it was still dark, he looked at his watch. It was about 4 A.M. He felt another body next to him. The dog had crawled closer and was sleeping next to him. CH looked around and saw that Joe was lying on the other side of the dog. Since it was October, daylight didn't come until about 6 or 7 A.M. CH reached out on patted the dog's head and shoulder, to which a tail began thumping up and down. CH whispered to the dog, "You know we need a name for you."

"I agree" whispered Joe, who was awake also.

"You slept out here, too?" queried CH. "It's pretty chilly."

"I wanted to keep the dog warm, then I saw you had the same idea." grinned Joe.

The two men tried to think of a name for the rescued dog. Then another medic named Howard came out of the tent and saw them, went back inside and came back with 3 cups of coffee. "You guys didn't really think you could keep this a secret, did you?" he said, as Joe and CH sipped the hot, black beverage.

"Nearly everybody knows about it. Where did you find him, and what is his name?"

"We were just trying to come up with a name." said Joe.

"Well, first we need to get him inside where it's warm, since he's no longer a secret." said CH.

So they picked up the dog and took him inside and laid him in a spot that was out of the way. Excitement filled the tent as the wounded men realized the dog was there. The patients who could get up had to look at him too. He wagged his tail for everybody.

CHAPTER 26

Finding a name for the dog became everyone's obsession. They all wanted to touch him. By the second night the dog was able to stand by himself. "Just so he doesn't tear out his stitches." cautioned Joe.

"Having that dog around seems to be good for morale." said CH.

"Yes, he's taking their minds off the war for a few minutes. That's got to be a good thing." replied Joe.

CH said, "Maybe we can have a contest to decide what to call him. He really does need a name, or he's going to start answering to Dog."

"Now that's a really good idea, CH, but you rescued him. We all know that you should have the final decision."

"I'm OK with it, especially if naming the dog will help morale. Let's do it!"

So CH and Joe told the patients they could name the dog, and it would be a contest. The patients would make a list of names, and everyone would vote on it, but CH would have the last word on the final decision.

Word came that the Brig. General needed CH, so he ran to his tent. "Come in, Corporal. I need your help." shouted the General. "Yes Sir," replied CH.

"I just got word that some prisoners are being sent to us. They'll be here any minute. There's a high ranking officer among them. We don't get too many of them, especially this early in our offensive." said the General excitedly.

Soon, the prisoners arrived and were sent into the tent, one at a time. CH interpreted for the General, with the assistant typing as fast as he could. The last prisoner was the officer.

He was asked the same questions as the others. CH's face never changed expression, as he quietly did his job. After the prisoner's were gone, CH said he wasn't sure that he trusted the officer's answers. "Then do what you do when you walk back to the prisoner compound. I trust your judgment," said the General.

When CH returned, he gave the information to the General. He went to the map and pointed out where the inconsistencies were. The assistant typist said he got it all down. The General made a phone call to his men at the front. Then he turned to CH and thanked him. "Son, I really appreciate your abilities. You probably saved some lives again today."

"Thank you Sir. I should get back to the hospital tent. It's dark now, so I need to search for our wounded." CH saluted, and headed back to get his medic pack. He spent the rest of the night hunting through bodies, looking for live soldiers.

There was a slight stench of gas, so he put on his gas mask. CH also put gas masks on the wounded who couldn't do it for themselves. Litter bearers seemed to be everywhere. Today had been a brutal battle. Dead and wounded were strewn as far as the eye could see.

At one point, CH came face to face with a German medic. The two men looked at each other for what seemed like an eternity. Even though both were armed, neither reached for their weapon. Then the German gave a salute to CH. He returned the salute, and they both went on with their jobs. CH headed back with a wounded soldier slung over his shoulder, and one that had succumbed to the gas, but was still able to walk, holding on to CH's coat. They reached the pickup point, and waited a few minutes for a horse-drawn ambulance to come and take them back to the aid station.

CH was exhausted, but he took time to sit and talk to the dog, and that's where he stayed until daylight. He was awakened by Joe kicking his boot. "You want some coffee?" CH reached for the cup and sipped it. "Wow! That's hot!" He sat up straight, so he wouldn't spill it on the dog.

Joe and CH started talking about the busy night. Joe said that the tent was full of wounded, and the trucks were late in coming to pick up the worst cases and take them to the hospital.

An hour later, the trucks came and loaded the severely wounded, and headed back to the field hospital. CH went back to the dog, sat down and promptly fell asleep again. Joe decided to let him sleep.

CHAPTER 27

Names for the dog poured in. CH, Joe and Howard were pretty much overwhelmed. Howard ventured a suggestion, "How about setting up a box for them to put the names in so we can have all the entries in one place?" "Hey that's a great idea!" said Joe, as he pulled paper of every size and shape from his pockets. "But where can we get a box?" They looked around inside and out, but no box.

Then CH, who had just returned with newly wounded said, "I know where there's a wooden box. The Brig. General has one or two. I'll see if we can use one. How long do you think this is going to take?"

"How about Friday?" answered Howard.

"Sounds great to me ." said Joe.

"Then Friday it is." replied CH. "I'll go ask the Brig. General. I need to talk to him about something anyway."

CH hurried over to the Brig. General's tent, and went inside. "Morning Sir." said CH as he saluted. The Brig. General replied "Morning to you too Corporal. How can I help you?"

"Well Sir, I found a wounded German Shepherd dog while I was out on the battle field a couple of days ago. He was a message carrier for the Germans. He's very friendly, and has won the hearts of all of the men at the aid station. We decided to have a contest to name him, and we need a box to put the entries in until Friday after 7PM. I was hoping you would lend us one of your empty boxes."

"HMMM, well let me see. You need a ballot box." said the Brig. General, as he picked up a box and handed it to CH. "Will this do?"

"Yes Sir. That will do just fine."

The General wrote something on a piece of paper, folded it, and put it in the box. "I hope that I can enter a name. When I was a boy, I had a dog with this name. He was a great dog. I have heard about your dog, and the good he is doing with the wounded soldiers. Wonderful, just Wonderful. They need a diversion from their suffering."

Yes Sir, that's how we all felt about it. I do have something else that I would like to ask.

"What is it, CH?"

"Well Sir, I was hoping there might be a way I could keep the dog, and take him home with me after the war. I've really grown attached to him, and him to me."

"I'll make some inquiries and get back to you, son." said the Brig. General'.

CH took the box back to the aid station. Joe put the names in it, and announced to everyone that they had until Friday evening to get their ballots in.

These were just some of the names entered so far:

Fritz	Happy	Fido
Lucky	Dough dog	Hoppie
Hans	Thor	Sarge
Shep	Pepper	Jack
Argonne	Blitz	Eddie
Mike	Spike	Buddy

By Friday evening, the box was full. The excitement of the contest had reached most of the American Division. and they all had a suggestion for the name of the dog. There were so many names that it was going to take several hours to go through them. Then they had to decide which one best fit the dog.

Meanwhile, the dog was getting better and stronger. He followed CH around the aid station, and did not attempt to run away.

He still favored his back leg some. Joe predicted that he would make a full recovery, and would eventually loose his limp. He was such a good-natured canine. He wanted to please everyone, but it was obvious that he was CH's dog.

CH began giving him commands, mostly in German. He responded to all the regular ones: sit, down, stay, come, and place. He was responding so well that CH began teaching him to go to Joe. After a few times of pointing to Joe, and saying "Find Joe.", Joe began hiding. The dog still found him He would put his nose down and track Joe anywhere. Seeing that, CH tried letting the dog sniff Howard's sock, then commanded him to "Find Howard," which he did.

Then Howard and Joe tried it, and it worked! So they tried having the dog sniff patients socks, or even a handkerchief, or anything with a scent on it, and sent him to find them. He found every one without hesitation. Then the wounded soldiers tried sending him back to the medics, and he did it!

CH tried putting something small in the dog's collar (which he had made from a belt) and sending him to find whoever was waiting for the object. He would then be sent back to either CH, Joe, or Howard. "This is what he was trained to do. Now he will do it for us!" exclaimed CH.

"He even understands our English commands. You need to have him track longer distances!" exclaimed the Brig. General, who had been standing just inside the tent watching for some time.

"He's absolutely amazing." He then handed CH his hanky, and walked back to his tent. CH waited almost a half an hour, then sent the dog to find the Brig. General.

A few minutes later, the dog came back with a message, "It worked!"

Everybody in the aid station cheered. Even the severely wounded were smiling through their pain. CH sent the dog to kiss each patient, which he did happily. And, Oh yes, they did find the perfect name for the German Shepherd, Buddy.

CHAPTER 28

It didn't take long for Buddy to adjust to his new name. Everyone was astonished at the intelligence of the shepherd. It seemed that anything they asked him to do, he did. Soon, he was following CH all over camp. He especially liked riding in the horse-drawn ambulances.

Howard, who was pretty inventive, made a harness-saddlebag contraption that would hold medical supplies or whatever was needed. He accepted it as though he was used to it. CH figured Buddy had one before, but it wasn't with him when he was rescued. The Brig. General delighted in pulling mail out of the saddlebags, or putting some in, and sending him on his way. Buddy was one bright moment in the midst of a horrible war.

CH was careful to tell Buddy to stay in the ambulance when he went to look for wounded soldiers. The dog really wanted to go with him. The fighting had pushed the enemy back a little more every day. The surge went forward.

It was mid October and snow was once again becoming a nuisance. Remembering the blizzards the Allies had encountered last year, CH was not looking forward to the long, cold, bitter winter in France.

On one particularly cold night which had seen especially heavy gunfire, ambulances, medics, and litter-bearers were nearly exhausted. They still pushed on into the deadly night. Snow had been falling softly on the dead and wounded doughboys. Downed trees and debris made it difficult to find life. CH went into areas he wasn't sure he could get back from, but he didn't want to leave even one man that he could possibly help.

The trusty litter-bearers seemed to be able to find him as he ministered bandages and aid to the mangled, but alive soldiers. He lifted tree limbs until his arms and legs trembled from exhaustion. He carried several wounded soldiers. Others who could walk, helped the litter-bearers carry others back to the ambulances. They filled ambulances as fast as they could, and gathered guns and ammo, which they loaded into the ambulances.

Enemy artillery was still pumping all kinds of big gunfire into the areas close to where the pickups were being made. The ambulance driver told CH that they could come back only one more time, as they pulled the flaps down over the guns. The horses were exhausted, and no motorized truck could come this far into the woods. CH and the other medics said okay, they would make one more sweep, and then call it a night.

CH headed back over the rough terrain, his hands and feet wet and cold. His toes were numb, and he ached all over, but he pressed on. He found another soldier who had been shot and lost part of his hand. The man could still walk. so CH directed him to the pickup place, after bandaging his hand.

When he was pretty sure he had reached everyone he could, he headed back toward to place where the litter-bearers were waiting for the last ambulance. He had picked up a few more guns, and reached the pickup point about the same time as the wounded soldier he had just bandaged.

They had to wait awhile for the ambulance. One soldier who had been severely wounded, died. They laid his body near the pickup point, knowing the body detail would pick him up in a few days. It was cold enough to preserve the bodies, so they could wait.

The ambulance finally came, and they loaded up. The driver said the horse was limping, so he was afraid to push too hard. CH was out of bandages, so he took one off the dead soldier, and wrapped it around the horse's bad leg, and said "I hope this helps."

Since the ambulance was not full, it wasn't a difficult ride back. It turned out the horse only had a slight sprain. He would be rested for a day or two, until he could work again. As soon as they all got back to the aid station, and logged in all the wounded soldiers' names, CH headed for his bedroll, and Buddy. The dog was really glad to see him, but no more glad than CH was to see the dog. They were sound asleep in minutes, Buddy's head on CH's chest.

CHAPTER 29

The next few days, CH divided his time between tending wounded, and interpreting for whomever needed him. He was driven in a motor vehicle when he went outside of the American Division. Buddy rode with him every time. Sometimes the Brig, General came along, if they had a conference with the other division officers.

CH translated when papers were found on a prisoner. His French was improving, and he even picked up on Arabic, although he couldn't read or write it. He worked with the Moroccan interpreter, and they learned some of each other's language. Before long, CH had memorized the maps, and would use that information when he went out in search of wounded soldiers.

The war seemed to be advancing at a more rapid pace. The Allies were pushing deeper into the Argonne Forest. What was once a lush green forest of unmistakable beauty, was fast becoming a decimated land of ruin. The unwitting wildlife were the innocent victims. The carnage of men and beasts was often lamented by French soldiers as they gazed at the aftermath of battle. But they pushed on. The Big Red 1 was making real headway. The powers that be were pleased, and hoping for a quick ending of this, "The War to End All Wars".

CH sat quietly with Buddy at his side. They had just come from a meeting with one of the other divisions. The consensus was that we need to make the next few days the hardest fought yet. Fresh troops were being sent to help.

Suddenly Buddy started barking. A wounded soldier came running out of nowhere, and flagged down the truck. He had on a French uniform, but didn't speak French very well. Immediately the guns were aimed at him. He fell to his knees and cried out in German "Please don't kill me! Please don't kill me!"

The guards jumped down and called CH to find out what this was all about. He calmly asked who the soldier was. By this time, the wounds were catching up with the young German, and he passed out. CH quickly dressed his wounds. He had been shot twice, once in the leg, and once in the head, losing one eye.

They had already put him in the back of the truck when he awoke, with CH sitting next to him. CH asked him in German why he had flagged them down, and why was he in a French uniform.

The young soldier asked for a drink of water. One of the guards handed CH a canteen, and CH gave him a drink.

The German said he wanted to surrender. He had been forced into the German army six months ago. He was a farmer, not a soldier. He had received no training, and was sent into combat barely able to load and fire a gun. He said his name was Werner, and he basically hid every time there was shooting. Everybody was so busy shooting at the Allies, that nobody noticed him cowering in the smoke-filled battleground.

As his battalion was being pushed back to where he was hiding, he was shot. He fell unconscious, and when he awoke, there were only dead soldiers around him. He realized he was now in Allied territory. He grabbed hold of a dead French soldier, and pulled his body into a bomb crater, where he changed clothes, except for his boots. It was about that time that he heard the truck passing by.

Werner was taken back to the aid station, and his wounds were tended to. CH stayed by his side, talking softly to him. He learned that Werner was 15 years old, and had been picked up when the Germans had made a sweep of villages and farms to recruit soldiers. Tears came into CH's eyes as he thought about Clifford. Clifford too had been torn from his family

CH advised Werner that he would be a prisoner of war, and sent back to the prison compound until the war was over. Werner thanked him, and drifted off to sleep.

CHAPTER 30

It was almost mid day, and the sounds of combat were deafening, even this far away. It was going to be an especially hard battle for our men. As CH lamented about the war, they were loading wounded soldiers into trucks to be transported to field hospitals. CH rode out with the last truck, because Werner was in it. Buddy sat by CH's side. The trucks wobbled along on the bumpy rut-filled roads. It took two hours to reach the first stop. The POW was looked at by a doctor from a near by city. He said to take Werner to the hospital where he would need surgery to "clean up" his head wound. Only the most basic first aid had been done at the aid station.

CH was fascinated with all the tools the doctors used. he explained what was being used at the aid station. The doctor wasn't surprised. He offered to put a box of supplies together for CH to take back to the medics. CH was so happy that he wanted to kiss the doctor! He didn't, but he nearly shook his hand off. "We have lost a lot of equipment, but that happens when we move often.

CH and Buddy watched as Werner was taken out of the truck, and placed in another truck. CH told the boy that he was being taken to a <u>real </u>hospital, and that everything would be okay. "Okay - what is this word?" queried Werner. An orderly who understood German explained everything to the young German. Werner had a hard time separating from CH and Buddy. He had attached himself to the first kind person that he came in contact with, but he knew now that it would be "okay".

CH got into the truck going back to the aid station. The doctor had kept his promise, and had two boxes full of medical implements and bandages for CH to take back. It was a good two hour trip back to the aid station. CH was excited about taking the implements back to Joe. Joe was the closest there was to a surgeon. He had been in his last year of residency when he joined the military, and his knowledge was put to good use at the aid station. Now there would be new instruments for Joe to use, not to mention the other medics who would learn from Joe how to use each piece of the equipment.

When they pulled up to the aid station, Joe, Howard and two other medics were waiting. CH handed the boxes to Joe, who excitedly took them inside to see what treasures CH had brought.

There were severely wounded waiting to be placed in the truck to go back to the hospital. As soon as they could, Joe and CH emptied the boxes. There were several sets of surgical equipment, each set rolled up and tied. When unrolled, there were pockets for each implement. This would make it easier to use them. Everything needed to be sterilized, so they got a big pot from the kitchen, and boiled everything. Joe said he felt ready for nearly anything. CH cautioned. "Be careful what you wish for."

There were only two other medics with surgical experience, and there were six sets of implements. Joe gave each man two sets, one to use, and one to sterilize. Within an hour Joe was working on a wounded soldier. The other two medics observed. They were learning on the job. Soon they would be using their own sets of implements.

It was getting late, and daylight was falling behind the distant hills. CH sent Buddy with a note to the Brig. General, to see if there was anything he needed him to do. Buddy came back with the message that the Division Allies had pushed the enemy back nearly a mile. That mile was a costly one. Many had fallen.

CH told Buddy to stay with the ambulance, then he started out on his nightly search. They search was hard-going, but he found several live soldiers on his first sweep. Rifle fire was unusually close. He got the soldiers back to where the litter bearers were able to take them on to the pickup place. As soon as he knew they were safe, he started out again. The area had so much smoke from rifle and heavy artillery, that it became hard to breath, and slowed his search.

And then it happened......Mustard Gas! A last desperate act on a horrible day. CH grabbed his mask, and began counting to three, as he put it on......But he didn't make it to three.

Today, October 24, 1918, the war ended for C. H. Engelbert.

EPILOGUE

Thanks to Buddy's tracking abilities, CH was located and brought back to the field hospital. He suffered from chemical burns, nerve damage, and was blinded in one eye.

When he awoke in the hospital, he couldn't move and his face was covered with cloth.

For a minute he feared he was back in the German hospital again. As he was trying to work out in his mind what was going on, whatever was holding him down moved. He realized it was Buddy!

Buddy was laying on his chest and face.

0-o-h-h Buddy! rasped CH as he hugged the dog with such relief. He was not a prisoner as he suspected, but in a field hospital instead.

On November 11, 1918, "The War To End All Wars" finally ended.

Thanks to the officers and friends who went to bat for CH, and helped him clear the German Shepherd for travel to the United States, Buddy was at his side.

Printed in the United States
By Bookmasters